Cambridge English: Business Higher 5

WITH ANSWERS

Official examination papers from University of Cambridge ESOL Examinations

CAMBRIDGE UNIVERSITY PRESS
Cambridge, New York, Melbourne, Madrid, Cape Town,
Singapore, São Paulo, Delhi, Tokyo, Mexico City

Cambridge University Press
The Edinburgh Building, Cambridge CB2 8RU, UK

www.cambridge.org
Information on this title: www.cambridge.org/9781107610873

© Cambridge University Press 2012

This publication is in copyright. Subject to statutory exception
and to the provisions of relevant collective licensing agreements,
no reproduction of any part may take place without the written
permission of Cambridge University Press.

First published 2012

Printed in the United Kingdom at the University Press, Cambridge

A catalogue record for this book is available from the British Library

ISBN 978-1-107-61087-3 Student's Book with answers
ISBN 978-1-107-61118-4 Audio CD
ISBN 978-1-107-66917-8 Self-study Pack

Cambridge University Press has no responsibility for the persistence or
accuracy of URLs for external or third-party internet websites referred to in
this publication, and does not guarantee that any content on such websites is,
or will remain, accurate or appropriate. Information regarding prices, travel
timetables and other factual information given in this work is correct at
the time of first printing but Cambridge University Press does not guarantee
the accuracy of such information thereafter.

Contents

Thanks and acknowledgements 4

Introduction 5

Test 1 Reading   22
          Writing   32
          Listening   34
          Speaking   38

Test 2 Reading   40
          Writing   50
          Listening   52
          Speaking   56

Test 3 Reading   58
          Writing   68
          Listening   70
          Speaking   74

Test 4 Reading   76
          Writing   86
          Listening   88
          Speaking   92

Key (including tapescripts and sample answers)
          Test 1   94
          Test 2   108
          Test 3   122
          Test 4   136

Speaking test interlocutor frames 151

Sample Answer Sheets 153

Thanks and acknowledgements

Book design by Peter Ducker MSTD

Cover design by David Lawton

The CD which accompanies this book was recorded at dsound, London.

Introduction

TO THE STUDENT

This book is for candidates preparing for the Cambridge English: Business Higher examination, also known as BEC Higher. It contains four complete tests based on past papers.

Cambridge English: Business

Cambridge English: Business is a suite of certificated tests which can be taken on various dates throughout the year at approved Cambridge centres. They are aimed primarily at individual learners who wish to obtain a business-related English language qualification, and provide an ideal focus for courses in Business English. Set in a business context, Cambridge English: Business examinations test English language, not business knowledge. The examinations are available at three levels – Preliminary, Vantage and Higher.

Cambridge English: Business is linked to the ALTE/Cambridge levels for language assessment, and to the Council of Europe's Framework of Reference for Languages. It is also aligned with the UK Qualifications and Curriculum Authority's National Standards for Literacy, within the National Qualifications Framework (NQF).

Business Exam	Equivalent Main Suite Exam	Council of Europe Framework Level	UK NQF Level
	Cambridge English: Proficiency *Certificate of Proficiency in English (CPE)*	C2 (ALTE Level 5)	
Business Higher	Cambridge English: Advanced *Certificate in Advanced English (CAE)*	C1 (ALTE Level 4)	Level 2*
Business Vantage	Cambridge English: First *First Certificate in English (FCE)*	B2 (ALTE Level 3)	Level 1
Business Preliminary	Cambridge English: Preliminary *Preliminary English Test (PET)*	B1 (ALTE Level 2)	Entry 3
	Cambridge English: Key *Key English Test (KET)*	A2 (ALTE Level 1)	

*This represents the level typically required for employment purposes to signify the successful completion of compulsory secondary education in the UK.

Business Higher

The Business Higher examination consists of four papers:

Reading	1 hour
Writing	1 hour 10 minutes
Listening	40 minutes (approximately)
Speaking	16 minutes

Introduction

Test of Reading (1 hour)

This paper consists of six parts with 52 questions, which take the form of two multiple-matching tasks, two multiple-choice tasks, a cloze test and an error identification task. Part 1 contains five short texts or a longer text divided into five sections, and Parts 2, 3, 4, 5 and 6 each contain one longer text. The texts are taken from newspapers, business magazines, business correspondence, books, leaflets, brochures, etc. They are all business-related, and are selected to test a wide range of reading skills and strategies.

Test of Writing (1 hour 10 minutes)

For this paper, candidates are required to produce two pieces of writing. For Part 1, they write a short report based on graphic input. For Part 2, they choose whether to write a short report, a piece of business correspondence or a proposal. Candidates are asked to write 120 to 140 words for Part 1 and 200 to 250 words for Part 2. Assessment is based on content, communicative achievement, organisation and language.

Test of Listening (approximately 40 minutes)

This paper consists of three parts with 30 questions, which take the form of a note-completion task, a multiple-matching task and a multiple-choice task. Part 1 contains a monologue in a work-related situation, Part 2 contains five very short monologues, and Part 3 contains one longer conversation between two or more people. The texts are audio recordings based on a variety of sources including interviews, face-to-face conversations and documentary features. They are all business-related, and are selected to test a wide range of listening skills and strategies.

Test of Speaking (16 minutes)

The Speaking test consists of three parts, which take the form of an interview section, a short presentation on a business topic, and a discussion. In the standard test format, candidates are examined in pairs by two examiners: an interlocutor and an assessor. The assessor awards a mark based on the following four criteria: Grammar and Vocabulary, Discourse Management, Pronunciation and Interactive Communication. The interlocutor provides a global mark for the whole test.

Marks and results

The four Higher papers total 120 marks, after weighting. Each paper is weighted to 30 marks. A candidate's overall grade is based on the total score gained in all four papers. It is not necessary to achieve a satisfactory level in all four papers in order to pass the examination. Every candidate is provided with a Statement of Results, which includes a graphical display of their performance in each paper. These are shown against the scale Exceptional – Good – Borderline – Weak and indicate the candidate's relative performance in each paper.

Introduction

TO THE TEACHER

Candidature

Each year Cambridge English: Business exams are taken by over 130,000 candidates throughout the world. Most candidates are either already in work or studying in preparation for the world of work.

Content, preparation and assessment

Material used throughout the exams is as far as possible authentic and free of bias, and reflects the international flavour of the examination. The subject matter should not advantage or disadvantage certain groups of candidates, nor should it offend in areas such as religion, politics or sex.

TEST OF READING

Part	Main Skill Focus	Input	Response	No. of Questions
1	Reading for gist and global meaning	Authentic business-related text – either a single text or five short, related texts (approx. 450 words in total)	Matching	8
2	Reading for structure and detail	Authentic business-related text (approx. 450–500 words) with sentence-length gaps	Matching	6
3	Understanding general points and specific details	Longer text based on authentic source material (approx. 500–600 words)	4-option multiple choice	6
4	Reading – vocabulary and structure	Single business-related text with primarily lexical gaps (approx. 250 words)	4-option multiple-choice cloze	10
5	Reading – structure and discourse features	Single business-related text with structure and discourse gaps (approx. 250 words)	Rational deletion Open cloze	10
6	Reading – understanding sentence structure; error identification	Short text (approx. 150–200 words). Identification of additional unnecessary words in text	Proof-reading	12

Reading Part One

This is a matching task. The text is approximately 450 words long, and is made up of five related short texts of authentic origin. Examples could be a set of related product descriptions, a set of advertisements (for instance, for different types of services), notices or messages, book or video reviews, short newspaper items on related topics. Texts may be edited, but the source is authentic. They are identified as texts A–E.

Introduction

There are eight statements, each of which is one sentence long, numbered 1–8. Each statement can be matched with only one of the texts. The candidate's task is to read the statement and then scan the texts for the one to which each statement applies. Candidates are tested on whether they can understand the language of the statement and relate it to the meaning of the text, which is expressed in different language.

Preparation
- Present students with sets of related short texts (e.g. job advertisements, hotel information, etc.) from newspapers, magazines, brochures;
- Longer texts may also be divided into sub-headed sections;
- Students should be encouraged to identify facts or ideas within each text, describing how the texts are similar and what differences they contain;
- The register or style of the task sentences is likely to differ from that of the texts, and students should be given practice in recognising the same information in different styles, e.g. by rewriting advertisements into objective prose;
- The task is designed to go beyond simple word-matching, and students will need to practise paraphrasing;
- Activities that help students to identify target information among otherwise superfluous text (e.g. choosing what to watch from TV listings) would be beneficial;
- Above all, students should treat the task as an example of information-processing skills which are frequently employed in social and professional life.

Reading Part Two

This is a gapped text with six sentence-length gaps. The text is about 450 to 500 words long, and comes from an authentic business-related source, although it may be edited. Sources include business articles from newspapers or magazines, books on topics such as management, or company literature such as annual reports. Candidates have to read the text and then identify the correct sentence to fill each gap from a set of eight sentences marked A–H. Sentence H is the example, and one other sentence is a distractor which does not fit any of the gaps. Understanding of not only the meaning of the text but some of the features of its structure is tested.

Preparation
- This task requires an overt focus on cohesion and coherence, to which many students may not be accustomed;
- It would be helpful for students to reassemble texts that have been cut up, discussing why texts fit together as they do;
- It would also be useful for students to discuss why sentences do or do not fit together;
- Students could benefit from altering the cohesion of texts to make sentences that do not fit together do so, and vice versa;
- Since culture affects discourse, including the order of argument development, discussions exploring this would be beneficial;
- The cut-and-paste functions of word-processing, where available, could be exploited for this task.

Reading Part Three

This task consists of a text accompanied by four-option multiple-choice items. The stem of a multiple-choice item may take the form of a question or an incomplete sentence. There are six items, which are placed after the text. The text is about 500 to 600 words long. Sources of original texts may be the general and business press, company literature, and books on topics such as management. Texts may be edited, but the source is authentic.

Preparation
- Multiple-choice questions are a familiar and long-standing type of test; here, they are used to test opinion and inference rather than straightforward facts;
- Correct answers are designed not to depend on simple word-matching, and students' ability to interpret paraphrasing should be developed;
- Students should be encouraged to pursue their own interpretation of relevant parts of the text and then check their idea against the options offered, rather than reading all the options first;
- It could be useful for students to be given perhaps one of the wrong options only, and for them to try to write the correct answer and another wrong option.

Reading Part Four

This task is a modified cloze: in other words, a gapped text in which the gaps are carefully chosen. There are ten multiple-choice items, most of which test vocabulary. The text is approximately 250 words long and is based on authentic source material of one of the text types listed above. The candidate's task is to choose the correct option, from the four available, to fill each gap.

Preparation
- It is important for students to appreciate that the correct answer in each case is correct in relation to the gap itself, rather than in relation to the other three options;
- It is worth emphasising that this task tests lexical and collocational knowledge, and that the best route to this knowledge is to read widely within the kinds of texts that the task employs;
- It is worth discussing what aspects of linguistic knowledge are tested (collocations, fixed phrases, register, etc.);
- It might be useful to give students gapped texts and have them produce alternative words which fit and which do not fit the gaps;
- Any vocabulary-building activity is likely to be helpful in preparing for this task.

Reading Part Five

This task is an open cloze: a gapped text in which the candidate has to supply the word to fill each gap. There are ten items. Gaps are formed by rational deletion, being chosen rather than being simply those which occur if (for example) every seventh word

Introduction

is deleted. The focus is on structure, and coherence/cohesion in the text. Items tested may include prepositions, auxiliary verbs, pronouns, conjunctions, etc. The text is based on authentic material, and it is approximately 250 words long. A title is usually included.

Preparation
- The kinds of words which are gapped may well correspond to the kinds of errors students make, and therefore discussion of photocopied examples of students' compositions could be helpful;
- Students should be encouraged to circle the word or words in the text that dictate what the answer will be, in order for them to see that such clues to the answer may be adjacent to the gap or several words distant;
- Students should brainstorm various likely words which might fit a particular gap, and then discuss why the ones that do not fit do not do so;
- Students could be given several possible answers for a gap and discuss why the correct answer is correct;
- This task tests grammatical and structural aspects of language, and any practice in these areas should be beneficial.

Reading Part Six

This is an error-correction or proof-reading task based on a text of about 150 to 200 words, with 12 items. Candidates identify additional or unnecessary words in a text. This task can be related to the authentic task of checking a text for errors, and suitable text types are therefore letters, publicity materials, etc. The text is presented with 12 numbered lines, which are the lines containing the items. Further lines at the end may complete the text, but these are not numbered.

Preparation
- Students should be reminded that this task represents a kind of editing that is common practice, even in their first language;
- Any work on error analysis is likely to be helpful for this task;
- It may well be that photocopies of students' own writing could provide an authentic source for practice;
- A reverse of the exercise (giving students texts with missing words) might prove beneficial.

Marks

One mark is given for each correct answer. The total score is then weighted to 30 marks for the whole Reading paper.

TEST OF WRITING

Part	Functions/Communicative Task	Input	Response	Register
1	e.g. describing or comparing figures from graphic input, making inferences	Rubric and graphic input	Short report (medium may be memo or email) (120–140 words)	Neutral/formal
2	Report: describing, summarising Correspondence: e.g. explaining, apologising, reassuring, complaining Proposal: describing, summarising, recommending, persuading	Rubric, possibly supplemented by brief input text, e.g. notice, advert	Candidates choose from report (medium could be memo or email) or business correspondence (medium may be letter, fax or email) or proposal (medium could be memo or email) (200–250 words)	Neutral/formal

For Higher, candidates are required to produce two pieces of writing:
- a short report based on graphic input;
- one of the following (of the candidate's choosing):
  - a report: the report will contain an introduction, main body of findings and conclusion; it is possible that the report may be delivered through the medium of a memo or an email;
  - a piece of business correspondence: this means correspondence with somebody outside the company (e.g. a customer or supplier) on a business-related matter, and the delivery medium may be a letter, fax or email;
  - a proposal: this has a similar format to a report but, unlike the report, the focus of the proposal is on the future, with the main focus being on recommendations for discussion; it is possible that the proposal may be delivered through the medium of a memo or an email.

Writing Part One

This is a guided writing task, in which the candidate produces a brief (120–140-word) report. The task provides a realistic situation in which it is necessary to analyse some sort of graphic input and express the information it conveys in words. Graphs, bar charts and pie charts of the type frequently used in the business pages of newspapers, company reports and brochures may provide a starting point. The graphic input is taken from an authentic source, but may be modified in the same way that a text may be edited. The rubric acts to amplify and clarify the situation, as well as making clear what the task involves.

Writing Part Two

In most parts of the Cambridge English: Business Writing tests, all candidates are required to perform the same task because there is no danger of individuals or groups of candidates being disadvantaged by that task. The exception is Higher Writing Part Two: in order to

Introduction

generate the range of language which is characteristic of this level of language learner, the task contains no input or minimal input, resulting in a relatively high background knowledge requirement from the candidate. In the absence of a choice of tasks, this would be likely to disadvantage some candidates, so a choice of tasks is given.

Candidates choose from three options: a report, a piece of business correspondence or a proposal. The task is supplied by the rubric, which provides an authentic reason for writing, and indicates who the piece of writing is being produced for. The input is therefore more detailed and specific than that of the traditional 'essay question' task type.

Preparing for the Writing paper

The first Writing task involves the kind of graphic input of information which is common in the business world, and students should be exposed to a wide range of examples of graphs and charts from newspapers, magazines, company literature, etc. The interpretation involved is the translating of the graphic input into prose, rather than the recommending of action. Students should have practice in the clear and concise presentation of written information. Specific vocabulary and phrasing should also be developed.

The second Writing task requires students to plan carefully in order to be able to produce successful answers. They should be given practice in considering:
- the target reader
- the purpose of writing
- the requirements of the format (letter, report, etc.)
- the main points to be addressed
- the approximate number of words to be written for each point
- suitable openings and closings
- the level of formality required.

Exposure to, and discussion of, as wide a range as possible of relevant texts would be beneficial.

Assessment

An impression mark is awarded to each piece of writing. Examiners look at four aspects of the candidate's writing: Content, Communicative Achievement, Organisation and Language.

Content focuses on how well the candidate has fulfilled the task, in other words if they have done what they were asked to do.
Communicative Achievement focuses on how appropriate the writing is and whether the appropriate register has been used.
Organisation focuses on the way the candidate put the piece of writing together, in other words if it is logical and ordered, and the punctuation is correct.
Language focuses on the use of vocabulary and grammar. This includes the range of language as well as how accurate it is.

For each of the criteria, the examiner gives a maximum of 5 marks. The band scores awarded are translated to a mark out of 10 for Part 1 and a mark out of 20 for Part 2. A total of 30 marks is available for Writing.

The general impression mark scheme is interpreted at Council of Europe Level C1.

Assessment Scale

C1	Content	Language	Organisation	Communicative Achievement
5	All content is relevant to the task. Target reader is fully informed.	Uses a range of everyday vocabulary appropriately, with occasional inappropriate use of less common lexis. Uses a range of simple and some complex grammatical forms with a good degree of control. Errors do not impede communication.	Text is generally well-organised and coherent, using a variety of linking words and cohesive devices.	Uses the conventions of the communicative task to hold the target reader's attention and communicate straightforward ideas.
4	*Performance shares features of Bands 3 and 5.*			
3	Minor irrelevances and/or omissions may be present. Target reader is on the whole informed.	Uses everyday vocabulary generally appropriately, while occasionally overusing certain lexis. Uses simple grammatical forms with a good degree of control. While errors are noticeable, meaning can still be determined.	Text is connected and coherent, using basic linking words and a limited number of cohesive devices.	Uses the conventions of the communicative task in generally appropriate ways to communicate straightforward ideas.
2	*Performance shares features of Bands 1 and 3.*			
1	Irrelevances and misinterpretation of task may be present. Target reader is minimally informed.	Uses basic vocabulary reasonably appropriately. Uses simple grammatical forms with some degree of control. Errors may impede meaning at times.	Text is connected using basic, high-frequency linking words.	Produces text that communicates simple ideas in simple ways.
0	Content is totally irrelevant. Target reader is not informed.	*Performance below Band 1.*		

Length of responses

Guidelines on length are provided for each task; responses which are too short may not have an adequate range of language and may not provide all the information that is required, while responses which are too long may contain irrelevant content and have a negative effect on the reader. These may affect candidates' marks on the relevant subscales.

Varieties of English

Candidates are expected to use a particular variety of English with some degree of consistency in areas such as spelling, and not for example switch from using a British spelling of a word to an American spelling of the same word.

Introduction

TEST OF LISTENING

Part	Main Skill Focus	Input	Response	No. of Questions
1	Listening for and noting specific information	Informational monologue	Gap-filling requiring limited written responses (i.e. no more than three words)	12
2	Listening to identify topic, context, function, speaker's opinion, etc.	Five short monologues linked by theme or topic, from five different speakers	Multiple matching	10
3	Listening for gist, specific information, attitudes, etc.	Conversation/interview/discussion between two or more people	3-option multiple choice	8

Listening Part One

This is a sentence-completion, gap-filling or note-taking task. The candidate has to supply only the key words of the answer, which will not be more than three words per item.

The spoken text lasts about two or three minutes and is a monologue. The text is heard twice. It is informational, and focuses on a series of identifiable facts. Topics might involve instructions, changes in arrangements or instructions, the programme for an event or meeting of some kind, or a presentation about a company. The setting for the task could be someone giving information over the telephone, or a speaker addressing a roomful of delegates at a conference or people on a training course.

Listening tasks may be based on recorded material taken from authentic sources or more usually on scripted material. There are 12 items, which are distributed evenly throughout the text, so that candidates have time to record their answers. Answers to items may be numbers or amounts of money, but these will not involve the candidate in any calculations. Items of information are tested in the same order in which the information occurs in the text.

Listening Part Two

This is a matching task based on five short extracts linked by theme or topic and spoken by five different speakers, in monologue form. The texts last a total of approximately three to four minutes.

There are two tasks for each of the five extracts. These tasks relate to the content and purpose of the extracts, and candidates are asked to do any combination of the following: identify speakers, interpret context, recognise the function of what is said, identify the topic, understand specific information, identify a speaker's opinion or feelings.

The series of extracts is heard twice, and candidates must attempt both tasks during this time. It is for the candidates to decide whether they choose to do the first task the first time they listen to the text, and the second task the second time, or whether to deal with the two tasks for each extract together. For each task, they have a list of eight options to choose from. Materials for this task are scripted, and relate to a business topic or situation.

Listening Part Three

This task consists of a dialogue, usually with two or more speakers. There are eight items, which are three-option multiple choice. The task relates to a topic of interest or concern in the world of work. The text is heard twice.

Preparing for the Listening paper

All listening practice should be helpful for students, whether authentic or specially prepared. In particular, discussion should focus on:
- the purpose of speeches and conversations or discussions
- the speakers' roles
- the opinions expressed
- the language functions employed
- relevant aspects of phonology such as stress, linking and weak forms, etc.

In addition, students should be encouraged to appreciate the differing demands of each task type. It will be helpful not only to practise the task types in order to develop a sense of familiarity and confidence, but also to discuss how the three task types relate to real-life skills and situations:
- the first is note-taking (and therefore productive), and students should reflect on the various situations in which they take notes from a spoken input; they should also be encouraged to try to predict the kinds of words or numbers that might go in the gaps;
- the second is a matching (with discrimination) exercise, and reflects the ability to interrelate information between reading and listening and across differing styles and registers;
- the third involves the correct interpretation of spoken input, with correct answers often being delivered across different speakers.

In all three tasks, successful listening depends on correct reading, and students should be encouraged to make full use of the pauses during the test to check the written input.

Marks

One mark is given for each correct answer, giving a total score of 30 marks for the whole Listening paper.

Introduction

TEST OF SPEAKING

Part	Format/Content	Time	Interaction Focus
1	Conversation between the interlocutor and each candidate Giving personal information; talking about present circumstances, past experiences and future plans, expressing opinions, speculating, etc.	About 3 minutes	The interlocutor encourages the candidates to give information about themselves and to express personal opinions.
2	A 'mini presentation' by each candidate on a business theme Organising a larger unit of discourse Giving information and expressing opinions	About 6 minutes	Each candidate is given prompts which they use to prepare and give a short talk on a business-related topic.
3	Two-way conversation between candidates followed by further prompting from the interlocutor Expressing and justifying opinions, speculating, comparing and contrasting, agreeing and disagreeing, etc.	About 7 minutes	The candidates are presented with a business-related situation to discuss. The interlocutor extends the discussion with further spoken prompts

The test is conducted by two Speaking examiners (an interlocutor and an assessor), with pairs of candidates. The interlocutor is responsible for conducting the Speaking test and is also required to give a mark for each candidate's performance during the whole test. The assessor is responsible for providing an analytical assessment of each candidate's performance and, after being introduced by the interlocutor, takes no further part in the interaction.

The Speaking test is designed for pairs of candidates. However, where a centre has an uneven number of candidates, the last three candidates will be examined together.

Speaking Part One

For this part of the test, the interlocutor asks the candidates questions on a number of personal or work-related subjects.

Speaking Part Two

In this part, each candidate's task is to choose one topic from a set of three, and to talk on it for about one minute. Candidates have one minute in which to prepare, and should use this time to make brief notes. While one candidate speaks, the other listens (and may make notes), after which they ask the candidate who gave the talk a question.

Candidates are again advised to keep in mind the business orientation of this test. It is wise to structure the one-minute talk, for example, as points, with an introduction and conclusion (however brief these must, of necessity, be), and to make the structure explicit when giving the talk in order to show some evidence of planning. Candidates should approach the task as if giving a presentation in a business environment.

Examples of topic areas for the individual Speaking task include the following: advertising, career planning, communications, customer relations, finance, health and safety, management (personnel, production, transport, etc.), marketing, recruitment, sales, technology, training and travel.

Speaking Part Three

This is a two-way collaborative task based on a prompt, which is given to both candidates. The prompt consists of several sentences stating a business-related situation followed by two or three discussion points. Candidates are given time to read the prompt and then they discuss the situation together.

Candidates need to approach the task as a simulation, imagining themselves in a work environment, faced with a real situation to discuss and on which they should try to reach some decisions. The opinions they express, however, are their own. They are not instructed, as in some kinds of role play, to assume particular attitudes or opinions.

Preparing for the Speaking test

Students should be made familiar with the seating arrangements and paired assessment procedures that the Speaking test employs. Any speaking practice should be of benefit, in particular paired and small-group work.

- For **Part One**, students should be familiar with the topics that the test covers. Activities designed to develop fluency will be of considerable benefit, as the students need to demonstrate as wide a range of language as possible within the time limits of the test. It should be noted not only that the test is designed to minimise the possibility of attempts to use rehearsed speech, but also that examiners will quickly identify it.
- For **Part Two,** they need to develop the ability to prepare effectively for the long turn they are required to take. They should be given help in developing the skill of long-turn-taking, and in building up a range of discourse features to make their speech both coherent and cohesive. It is also important for them to listen to each other's talks, and be ready to ask relevant questions.
- For **Part Three,** students will benefit from practice in this kind of simulation, where they have to put themselves into a work environment, and collaborate to discuss and decide issues. They should be helped to build up a range of resources for turn-taking and the general negotiating of ideas and opinions.

Introduction

Assessment

Throughout the test candidates are assessed on their own individual performance and not in relation to the other candidate. They are assessed on their language skills, not on their personality, intelligence or knowledge of the world. Candidates must, however, be prepared to develop the conversation and respond to the tasks in an appropriate way.

Candidates are awarded marks by two examiners; the assessor and the interlocutor. The assessor awards marks by applying performance descriptors from the Analytical Assessment scales for the following criteria:

Grammatical Resource

This refers to the accurate use of a range of grammatical forms.

Lexical Resource

This refers to the use of a range of appropriate vocabulary, to talk about a range of topics.

Discourse Management

This refers to the extent, relevance and coherence of each candidate's contributions. Candidates should be able to construct clear stretches of speech which are easy to follow. The length of their contributions should be appropriate to the task, and what they say should be related to the topic with clearly organised ideas.

Pronunciation

This refers to the intelligibility of contributions at word and sentence levels. Candidates should be able to produce utterances that can easily be understood, and which show control of intonation, stress and individual sounds to help convey meaning.

Interactive Communication

This refers to the ability to use language to achieve meaningful communication. Candidates should be able to initiate and respond appropriately according to the task and conversation, and also to use interactive strategies to maintain and develop the communication whilst negotiating towards an outcome.

Introduction

C1	Grammatical Resource	Lexical Resource	Discourse Management	Pronunciation	Interactive Communication
5	• Maintains control of a wide range of grammatical forms.	• Uses a wide range of appropriate vocabulary to give and exchange views on familiar and unfamiliar topics.	• Produces extended stretches of language with ease and with very little hesitation. • Contributions are relevant, coherent and varied. • Uses a wide range of cohesive devices and discourse markers.	• Is intelligible. • Phonological features are used effectively to convey and enhance meaning.	• Interacts with ease, linking contributions to those of other speakers. • Widens the scope of the interaction and negotiates towards an outcome.
4	*Performance shares features of Bands 3 and 5.*				
3	• Shows a good degree of control of a range of simple and some complex grammatical forms.	• Uses a range of appropriate vocabulary to give and exchange views on familiar and unfamiliar topics.	• Produces extended stretches of language with very little hesitation. • Contributions are relevant and there is a clear organisation of ideas. • Uses a range of cohesive devices and discourse markers.	• Is intelligible. • Intonation is appropriate. • Sentence and word stress is accurately placed. • Individual sounds are articulated clearly.	• Initiates and responds appropriately, linking contributions to those of other speakers. • Maintains and develops the interaction and negotiates towards an outcome.
2	*Performance shares features of Bands 1 and 3.*				
1	• Shows a good degree of control of simple grammatical forms, and attempts some complex grammatical forms.	• Uses appropriate vocabulary to give and exchange views, but only when talking about familiar topics.	• Produces extended stretches of language despite some hesitation. • Contributions are relevant and there is very little repetition. • Uses a range of cohesive devices.	• Is intelligible. • Intonation is generally appropriate. • Sentence and word stress is generally accurately placed. • Individual sounds are generally articulated clearly.	• Initiates and responds appropriately. • Maintains and develops the interaction and negotiates towards an outcome with very little support.
0	*Performance below Band 1.*				

Introduction

The interlocutor awards a mark for overall performance using a Global Achievement scale.

C1	Global Achievement
5	• Handles communication on a wide range of topics, including unfamiliar and abstract ones, with very little hesitation. • Uses accurate and appropriate linguistic resources to express complex ideas and concepts and produce extended discourse that is coherent and easy to follow.
4	*Performance shares features of Bands 3 and 5.*
3	• Handles communication on a range of familiar and unfamiliar topics, with very little hesitation. • Uses accurate and appropriate linguistic resources to express ideas and produce extended discourse that is generally coherent.
2	*Performance shares features of Bands 1 and 3.*
1	• Handles communication on familiar topics, despite some hesitation. • Organises extended discourse but occasionally produces utterances that lack coherence, and some inaccuracies and inappropriate usage occur.
0	*Performance below Band 1.*

Assessment for Higher is based on performance across all parts of the test, and is achieved by applying the relevant descriptors in the assessment scales.

Grading and results

Grading takes place once all scripts have been returned to Cambridge ESOL and marking is complete. This is approximately five weeks after the examination. There are two main stages: grading and awards.

Grading

The four papers total 120 marks, after weighting. Each paper represents 25% of the total marks available. The grade boundaries (A, B, C, B2) are set using the following information:
- statistics on the candidature
- statistics on the overall candidate performance
- statistics on individual items, for those parts of the examination for which this is appropriate (Reading and Listening)
- the advice of the Principal Examiners, based on the performance of candidates, and on the recommendation of examiners where this is relevant (Writing)
- comparison with statistics from previous years' examination performance and candidature.

A candidate's overall grade is based on the total score gained in all four papers. It is not necessary to achieve a satisfactory level in all four papers in order to pass the examination.

Awards

The Awarding Committee deals with all cases presented for special consideration, e.g. temporary disability, unsatisfactory examination conditions, suspected collusion, etc. The Committee can decide to ask for scripts to be re-marked, to check results, to change grades, to withhold results, etc. Results may be withheld because of infringement of regulations or because further investigation is needed. Centres are notified if a candidate's results have been scrutinised by the Awarding Committee.

Results

Exceptional candidates sometimes show ability beyond C1 level. Candidates who achieve grade A receive the Business English Certificate Higher stating that they demonstrated ability at Level C2. Candidates who achieve grade B or C receive the Business English Certificate Higher at Level C1. Candidates whose performance is below C1 level, but falls within Level B2, receive a Cambridge English certificate stating that they have demonstrated ability at B2 level. Candidates whose performance falls below Level B2 do not receive a certificate.

Further information

For more information about the Cambridge English: Business tests or any other Cambridge ESOL examination write to:

University of Cambridge ESOL Examinations
1 Hills Road
Cambridge
CB1 2EU
United Kingdom

Tel: +44 1223 553997
Fax: +44 1223 553621
email: ESOLHelpdesk@ucles.org.uk
website: www.CambridgeESOL.org

In some areas, this information can also be obtained from the British Council.

Test 1

READING 1 hour

PART ONE

Questions 1–8

- Look at the statements below and at the extracts from five job advertisements on the opposite page.
- Which advertisement (**A, B, C, D** or **E**) does each statement **1–8** refer to?
- For each statement **1–8**, mark one letter (**A, B, C, D** or **E**) on your answer sheet.
- You will need to use some of these letters more than once.
- There is an example at the beginnings (**0**).

Example:

0 This company is offering a job only on a temporary basis.

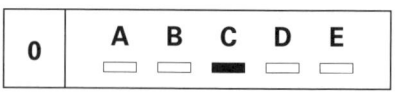

1 This company is known for dealing with problems quickly.

2 This company plans to take over other companies.

3 This company has as its clients some of the country's leading companies.

4 This company is not turning out as many goods as it could sell.

5 The person appointed to this post will deliver assistance to other companies.

6 This company wants to change the main focus of its attention.

7 This company's goods are expensive.

8 The person appointed to this job will have to show an ability to deal with ever-changing market conditions.

A

HEAD OF PRODUCTION
Success for this £40 million food production plant has come as a result of clear national market focus, coupled with quality products commanding premium prices. Demand continues to outstrip the ability to produce and new product lines have been enthusiastically received by the market place. To ensure that the business meets its demanding customer requirements in a well-controlled and professional fashion, a Head of Production is now needed to install good manufacturing practices and to ensure that the production staff are moulded more positively into a cohesive and responsive unit.

B

OPERATIONS MANAGER
We are a major stationery company. After years of impressive success in ground-breaking new products and customer relationship development, our present objective is to drive manufacturing processes higher up the agenda and we are now committed to manufacturing innovation. We wish, therefore, to appoint a Senior Operations Manager to impart the very latest in manufacturing development. Drive, enthusiasm and a passion for excellence are required, as is the ability to win a similar response from colleagues at all levels.

C

PROJECT MANAGER
We are seeking to appoint a Project Manager to work on a two-year contract with the fish processing industry. Applicants must have a degree in food science or a business discipline with a minimum of three years' experience, preferably in the seafood industry, and must be able to demonstrate an understanding of the current issues facing the fish processing industry. Duties will include leading a small team of researchers, assessing the needs of client companies and providing them with support, primarily through the organisation of technical workshops.

D

MANAGING DIRECTOR
We are an international packaging and printing group and have ambitious plans for future expansion both through organic growth and by acquisition. We are now seeking a successor to our present Managing Director who is due to retire in three months' time. The successful candidate will have to display technical competence in the industry and will have a demonstrable track record of managing a high-technology business. The new MD will be expected to build on our enviable blue-chip customer base through secure and profitable business-development activities.

E

HEAD OF CUSTOMER SERVICE
We are looking for someone with team management, database and process development skills to head our customer-service department. The person appointed will be responsible for managing operational delivery and performance. He or she will have to demonstrate experience in the management of fluctuating supply and demand situations. The company, a leader in the provision of services to businesses in the telecommunications sector, has a strong reputation for quality and speed of solution delivery. We are poised to implement an explosive growth plan and are targeted to treble in size within five years.

Test 1

PART TWO

Questions 9–14

- Read this text from an article about job interviews.
- Choose the best sentence from the opposite page to fill each of the gaps.
- For each gap (**9–14**), mark one letter (**A–H**) on your Answer Sheet.
- Do not use any letter more than once.
- There is an example at the beginning (**0**).

Interviewing on screen

The problems of global recruitment are disappearing rapidly. The reason for this lies in the technology that could redefine the traditional job interview. (**0**) ....*H*..... These give them access to the global recruitment market, enabling them to interview and assess their choice of candidates on screen, for example via video-conference link, CD-ROM display or electronic file transfer.

The development of the use of technology as a method of recruitment has brought considerable benefits to recruitment practices. For example, it means great savings in terms of both time and the travel budget. (**9**) .... One problem with face-to-face interviews is that body language is bound to play an important part in them. (**10**) .... This necessarily leads to an inherent unfairness in such interviews. Putting distance between candidate and interviewer with the use of a video camera can help to overcome this problem as body language will be less obvious. (**11**) .... It could prove an unfair advantage, or possibly disadvantage, if used only with those unable to attend a face-to-face interview.

A great deal has been made in recent years of NLP (neuro-linguistic programming), which includes the science of body language and its value in job interviews. (**12**) .... Others, however, reject the new technology simply because they are afraid of it. The benefits of technology, though, are too great to ignore, when one considers that the best person for a particular job may decide not to attend an interview if he or she has to travel a considerable distance.

Appointing senior executives is increasingly seen as a global business. Companies which intend to select candidates for jobs from a wider pool will have little choice but to bear the cost of overseas travel to conventional interviews, or to embrace the new technology. (**13**) .... Inevitably, companies will be seeking more cost-effective ways of recruiting quality candidates, and for this, virtual interviewing may offer a solution.

The greatest value of face-to-face interviews is at the stage of final selection. (**14**) .... Nevertheless, there are many positive aspects of using technology as a recruitment tool. Times are changing, and unless the die-hards who ignore new technology change with them, they may find themselves left behind.

24

Example: 0 | A B C D E F G H

A At the same time, the economic climate suggests that there is a very real prospect of leaner budgets in future.

B We are instinctively inclined to feel more positive to people who are similar to us.

C However, some experts feel that the main advantage of on-screen interviewing is that it addresses flaws in the conventional interview.

D For this reason there will always be a place for them.

E For some posts, applicants may be able to choose between a face-to-face interview and an on-screen interview.

F Some people in industry consider this to be a far more reliable approach to selection than a high-tech interview.

G But for it to be completely fair, the on-screen method would have to be used with all candidates.

H Employers now have at their disposal a range of communication tools.

PART THREE

Questions 15–20

- Read the following article about different-sized management consultancies and the questions on the opposite page.
- For each question (**15–20**), mark one letter (**A, B, C** or **D**) on your Answer Sheet.

A few years ago, when Carol Nichols arrived as head of human resources with NVCT, the fast-expanding telecoms and software services company, she knew that from day one working with management consultancy firms would be an integral part of her role. 'I had already decided on the kind of consultancies I wanted to employ,' she says. 'When I started, I was pretty much a one-woman department. So it was important for me to form partnerships to help me support the growth of the department and the company. What I wanted was smaller consultancies with whom I could establish personal relationships – firms which would grow with us, and be flexible enough to respond to our changing needs.'

Paul Eden, Managing Director of NVCT, confirms the desirability of smaller consultancies. 'Larger firms have a tendency to use one person to sell, and another to deliver, with the result that clients may not really know who or what they are buying. With a smaller firm, you are buying the consultant as much as the product – the person rather than the brand.'

Penny White, financial services group Interco's Head of Strategic Management, highlights other advantages of the smaller consultancy. 'A smaller consultancy recognises that it cannot do everything, and is much more willing to work with other preferred consultants for the good of the client,' she says. 'And on fees, smaller consultancies can be less rigid and more cost-effective, simply because their overheads are lower. That is not to say that they need to undercut to win business, but part of a small consultancy's strategy must be to thoroughly investigate how to add value to everything it does. Larger consultancies are gaining expertise in business psychology and applying it to running change programmes, but they still tend to bring in their own team to implement projects, which means that when they move on, the know-how goes with them, leaving the client with a knowledge vacuum, not the integrated training that small firms, in particular, really need.'

But the larger consultancies do have their advocates. Bill Dawkins, editor of *Consultancy Today*: 'One area where the industry giants have an edge is where major global companies require a standardised service across a number of different countries. Such clients are frequently spending substantial sums of money in consulting engagements and, not surprisingly, they are seeking the reassurance of a recognised and respected brand which they know they can trust to deliver.'

When it comes to choosing which kind of consultancy to use, there is no right or wrong in any absolute sense. By their very nature, smaller entrants are able to move more swiftly than the larger firms. But the question is whether they have the necessary substance and track record behind them to see larger-scale programmes through. Choose a smaller consultancy for pilot implementations where you want 'look and see' solutions in a short space of time. Then turn to a larger firm for full implementation and transformation programmes. Increasingly, the choice between big and small is not mutually exclusive, but complementary. The two often find themselves working together on the same project – creating a combination neither of them can achieve on its own.

15 Carol Nichols preferred to use smaller consultancies because

- **A** she had previous experience of them.
- **B** they could develop alongside her company.
- **C** she would be able to have control over them.
- **D** they would improve her department's reputation.

16 Paul Eden says one advantage of smaller consultancies is that

- **A** clients benefit from continuous individual contact.
- **B** they have a clearer understanding of clients' brands.
- **C** clients feel they get a better return on their investment.
- **D** they are able to sell their ideas to clients more effectively.

17 Penny White points out that smaller consultancies can

- **A** be flexible about co-operating with other firms.
- **B** spend time researching a wide range of issues.
- **C** provide useful introductions to other firms.
- **D** advise firms on ways to reduce overheads.

18 Penny White says that larger consultancies do not

- **A** train their consultants to work with smaller companies.
- **B** appreciate the function of psychology in business.
- **C** deliver the results that projects are set up to achieve.
- **D** transfer their expertise fully to their clients.

19 According to Bill Dawkins, larger consultants

- **A** are able to pass on economies of scale to clients.
- **B** have a deeper understanding of industrial issues.
- **C** represent a more secure investment for some clients.
- **D** differentiate their advice according to country.

20 The writer concludes by recommending using smaller consultancies

- **A** in situations requiring quick results.
- **B** for monitoring projects' progress.
- **C** in conjunction with each other.
- **D** for the finer details of projects.

PART FOUR

Questions 21–30

- Read the article below about pricing policies.
- Choose the correct word to fill each gap from **A, B, C** or **D** on the opposite page.
- For each question **(21–30)**, mark one letter (**A, B, C** or **D**) on your Answer Sheet.
- There is an example at the beginning (**0**).

Pricing policies

Whenever a product or service is made (**0**) .... for sale, one of the most important (**21**) .... to be made is the one related to the price to be charged. To have no coherent policy (**22**) .... price - merely to 'think of a number' - is to (**23**) .... trouble.

The basic point as far as pricing is (**24**) .... is to answer the question, '(**25**) .... what level should we pitch our prices?' A relatively high price (in comparison to the competition) (**26**) .... that the product has something special about it not found in the other products. In other words, the customer is expected to pay a (**27**) .... for the extra-special qualities to be found in the product. This also applies to services like any form of maintenance or repair work. Unfortunately, it is a well-established economic law that the higher the price, the lower the (**28**) .... sold. Nonetheless, both ends of the market can be equally profitable.

The question of discounts is important too. Some organisations offer discounts out of (**29**) .... , while others never give any kind of discount. A 'quantity discount' can attract customers: the more they buy, the lower the unit price. 'Prompt-payment discounts' are another (**30**) .... to the customer (usually retailers), whereby if payment is made quickly (say, within ten days), the amount payable is less than it would normally be.

28

Example:

　　A　available　　B　convenient　　C　appointed　　D　obtainable

| 0 | **A** ▬ **B** ☐ **C** ☐ **D** ☐ |

21	**A** decisions	**B** considerations	**C** conclusions	**D** resolutions
22	**A** relating	**B** observing	**C** regarding	**D** accounting
23	**A** appeal	**B** welcome	**C** request	**D** invite
24	**A** implicated	**B** concerned	**C** included	**D** referred
25	**A** At	**B** To	**C** By	**D** With
26	**A** expresses	**B** marks	**C** exhibits	**D** indicates
27	**A** premium	**B** bonus	**C** commission	**D** reward
28	**A** mass	**B** volume	**C** bulk	**D** capacity
29	**A** practice	**B** course	**C** procedure	**D** habit
30	**A** inducement	**B** motive	**C** influence	**D** provocation

PART FIVE

Questions 31–40

- Read the article below about the importance of the office environment.
- For each question (31–40), write one word in CAPITAL LETTERS on your Answer Sheet.
- There is an example at the beginning (0).

Example: 0 A N

Beautiful is best

Is your office (0) .... attractive and comfortable place? Is it specifically designed to ensure that whatever stresses you encounter in the course of your work, your surroundings make life just that little bit (31) .... bearable? (32) .... you greeted every morning by cut flowers, the smell of freshly-brewed coffee and a colour scheme that (33) .... easy on the eye? Or do you have to settle for a desk covered with the pen marks of numerous former employees and a stationery cupboard that can be opened only with a pickaxe?

If the second scenario sounds more familiar, you are by (34) .... means alone. A recent survey found that 38% of employees feel the interior design of the office they work in prevents them from performing (35) .... the best of their abilities.

Many employers refuse to entertain the thought of improving and updating their offices (36) .... of the costs involved. In the long run, however, it might be unwise to be too tight-fisted (37) .... it comes to employees' comfort. The working environment (38) .... a direct effect on productivity, and 78% of bosses (39) .... responded to the survey agreed that a pleasant office is a major influence in attracting and retaining good-quality workers. Employee under-performance can not only spell financial loss; (40) .... also fuels personal frustration when the employee feels unfulfilled. And it's highly likely that the dissatisfied secretary will look to greener pastures – or cleaner offices.

Reading

PART SIX

Questions 41–52

- Read the text below about the hotel industry.
- In most of the lines (**41–52**) there is one extra word. It is either grammatically incorrect or does not fit in with the meaning of the text. Some lines, however, are correct.
- If a line is correct, write **CORRECT** on your Answer Sheet.
- If there is an extra word in the line, write **the extra word** in CAPITAL LETTERS on your Answer Sheet.
- The exercise begins with two examples (**0**) and (**00**).

Examples:

| 0 | W | I | L | L | | | |

| 00 | C | O | R | R | E | C | T |

Poor support for hotel students

0 Is there anyone in the hotel industry who will, instead of just complaining that they

00 can't find reliable, qualified staff, not to mention retain them, is actually prepared

41 to help students with continued professional development? At present time I'm an

42 associate member of a professional body in the hotel management. In order to

43 upgrade to full membership, I decided how to undertake the Professional Certificate.

44 As part of the course, I had requirement to complete an assignment on front-office

45 operations. This seemed straightforward, but I couldn't yet find one establishment

46 that was prepared to allow me to visit and gather the information I required. Some of

47 the 12 hotels I contacted, only two actually had the decency to explain that 'normally

48 it would be OK', but at the moment they couldn't spare the time or staff. Just as for

49 the rest, it was simply 'No'. Would someone please tell to me, and all the other

50 dedicated hospitality professionals out there who are trying to further on their career

51 prospects via continued professional development, exactly how we attain the

52 qualifications that the industry requires us, when the industry seems unwilling to help?

Test 1

WRITING   1 hour 10 minutes

PART ONE

Question 1

- The chart below shows the increase in a country's industrial output from 2009 to 2011, according to type of industry.
- Using the information from the chart, write a short **report** comparing the annual percentage increases in industrial output in the three categories of industry during the period.
- Write **120–140** words.

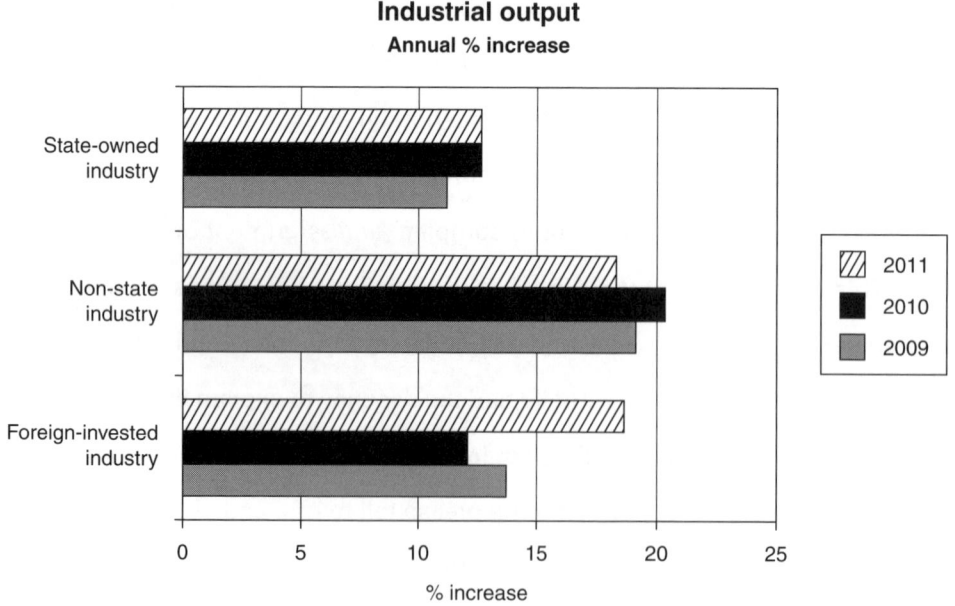

PART TWO

Write an answer to **one** of the questions **2–4** in this part. Write your answer in **200–250** words.

Question 2

- For an experimental period, your company has operated a scheme allowing certain employees in your department to work from home for part of the week. The Managing Director has asked you to write a report on the scheme.
- Write the **report** for the Managing Director:
    - explaining why it was decided to allow some staff to work from home
    - giving details of how the scheme operated
    - saying what the positive and/or negative aspects of the scheme have been
    - making a recommendation concerning the future of the scheme.

Question 3

- You have recently had a number of problems with a local company which supplies you with goods for your workplace. You have been asked to write a letter of complaint to the supplier about the situation.
- Write your **letter** to the supplier:
    - referring to the goods your company regularly buys from them
    - describing the various problems you have had
    - explaining how the situation might be dealt with
    - stating what will happen if the situation does not improve.

Question 4

- The Training Director of the company you work for is considering hiring a business training consultancy to provide the following courses: Appraising Staff, Software Applications and Giving Effective Presentations. You have been asked to write a proposal for the Training Director giving your views on these courses.
- Write a **proposal** for the Training Director:
    - saying which course you would like to attend and why
    - explaining how another of the courses would benefit one of your colleagues
    - advising against running one of the courses.

Test 1

LISTENING   Approximately 40 minutes (including 10 minutes' transfer time)

PART ONE

Questions 1–12

- You will hear the head of recruitment at Buyright Supermarkets plc talking to a group of job applicants who are attending the company's assessment centre.
- As you listen, for questions **1–12**, complete the notes using up to three words or a number.
- After you have listened once, replay the recording.

Buyright Supermarkets Assessment Centre

Briefing notes

1 Buyright have invited .... people to attend the assessment centre.

2 The discussion groups will have to solve a problem connected with ....

3 In the team challenges, everyone will have a chance to ....

4 The interviews will concentrate on the participants' ....

5 The participants should already have prepared their ....

6 In one of the simulations, participants will deal with a staff member who has been accused of ....

7 The four groups have each been given .... of different colours.

8 After this talk, the participants will be given the timetable of ....

9 Before dinner there will be a .... in the West Room.

10 The participants will be able to put questions to a panel of .... managers.

11 Ten people will be selected for the ....

12 Participants will find an expenses claim form in their ....

PART TWO

Questions 13–22

- You will hear five different people comparing their last job with their present job.
- For each extract, there are two tasks. For Task One, choose the reason the speaker gives for leaving their last job from the list **A–H**. For Task Two, decide what has surprised them about their new job.
- After you have listened once, replay the recording.

Task One – Reason for leaving

- For questions **13–17**, match the extracts with the reasons given by the speaker, listed **A–H**.
- For each extract, decide on the appropriate reason.
- Write one letter (**A–H**) next to the number of the extract.

13	Speaker 1	A	low pay
		B	long hours
14	Speaker 2	C	heavy responsibility
15	Speaker 3	D	unpleasant superior
		E	poor promotion prospects
16	Speaker 4	G	firm heading for trouble
		F	initiative not appreciated
17	Speaker 5	H	excessive travel

Task Two – Surprise

- For questions **18–22**, match the extracts with what has surprised each speaker about their new job, listed **A–H**.
- For each extract, choose what surprised each speaker.
- Write one letter (**A–H**) next to the number of the extract.

18	Speaker 1	A	the chance to develop ideas
		B	the excellent holiday entitlement
19	Speaker 2	C	the good pension scheme
20	Speaker 3	D	the generous bonuses
		E	the friendliness of the staff
21	Speaker 4	F	the amount of travelling
		G	the pleasant surroundings
22	Speaker 5	H	colleagues' positive attitude to the firm

35

Test 1

PART THREE

Questions 23–30

- You will hear Mark Finch, a well-known business consultant, speaking to a group of business people at a seminar.
- For each question (**23–30**), mark one letter (**A**, **B** or **C**) for the correct answer.
- After you have listened once, replay the recording.

23 Mark says it's important when starting up a business to

    A   have enough capital for the first two years.
    B   employ properly qualified staff.
    C   carry out effective research in the area.

24 What warning does Mark give?

    A   New businesses always take a long time to become successful.
    B   Trends in service industries often change very rapidly.
    C   People starting businesses must limit the hours they work.

25 What problem did the energy company have with its complaints system?

    A   Customers were critical of the computer system.
    B   Staff had not received sufficient computer training.
    C   The computers frequently broke down.

26 From his experience at the energy company, Mark says managers need to have

    A   effective communication with workers.
    B   more advice when choosing computer systems.
    C   experience of dealing with complaints directly.

27 In the car repair company, workers most wanted

    A   recognition of their work.
    B   a monthly newsletter.
    C   information about company aims.

28 What main benefit does Mark say came from reducing staff turnover?

    A   The company could stop providing training courses.
    B   Each mechanic carried out more work.
    C   There was less need for company advertising.

Listening

29 What is Mark's advice to the kitchen equipment company about its new product?

- **A** Increase the profit margin.
- **B** Reduce delivery costs.
- **C** Improve sales skills.

30 What does Mark say about stress?

- **A** Effective time management prevents stress.
- **B** Stress can improve personal performance.
- **C** Stress is on the increase in business.

> **You now have 10 minutes to transfer your answers to your Answer Sheet.**

Test 1

SPEAKING   16 minutes

SAMPLE SPEAKING TASKS

PART ONE

In this part, the interlocutor asks questions to each of the candidates in turn. You have to give information about yourself and express personal opinions.

PART TWO

In this part of the test, you are asked to give a short talk on a business topic. You have to choose one of the topics from the three below and then talk for about one minute. You have one minute to prepare your ideas.

> A **Sales:** the importance of reassuring customers about the security of internet transactions
>
> B **Business planning:** the factors involved in deciding whether to relocate a retail business
>
> C **Finance:** the importance of the role of the external auditor in financial management

PART THREE

In this part of the test, you are given a discussion topic. You have 30 seconds to look at the task prompt, an example of which is below, and then about three minutes to discuss the topic with your partner. After that, the examiner will ask you more questions related to the topic.

For **two** candidates

> **International Business Conference**
>
> The pharmaceutical company you work for is keen to participate in an international conference abroad. You have been asked to make recommendations about the company's participation.
>
> Discuss and decide together:
>
> - how to select members of staff to represent the company at the conference
> - what practical arrangements would need to be made by the company before the conference.

For **three** candidates

International Business Conference

The pharmaceutical company you work for is keen to participate in an international conference abroad. You have been asked to make recommendations about the company's participation.

Discuss and decide together:

- how to select members of staff to represent the company at the conference
- what practical arrangements would need to be made by the company before the conference
- how the company should respond after the conference to interest shown in its products.

Follow-on questions

- Would you like to take part in an international business conference? (Why?/Why not?)
- In what ways do you think international conferences benefit a company? (Why?)
- What are the benefits for staff of attending international conferences? (Why?)
- What advantages are there for the city where an international conference is held? (Why?)
- Do you think conferences will continue to be an effective means of making business contacts? (Why?/Why not?)

Test 2

READING 1 hour

PART ONE

Questions 1–8

- Look at the statements below and at the five newspaper items about different companies on the opposite page.
- Which company (**A, B, C, D** or **E**) does each statement (**1–8**) refer to?
- For each statement (**1–8**), mark one letter (**A, B, C, D** or **E**) on your Answer Sheet.
- You will need to use some of these letters more than once.
- There is an example at the beginning (**0**).

Example:

0 This company has sold off some of its brands.

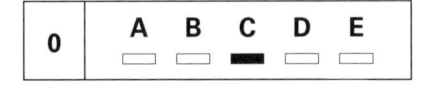

0	A	B	C	D	E
			■		

1   Shares in this company have stopped rising in value.

2   This company has again revised its growth targets downwards.

3   A problem experienced by this company has led to a change of personnel.

4   Suppliers may refuse to charge this company less for their goods.

5   A period of rapid growth immediately preceded a fall in this company's share price.

6   This company's reputation differs from that of its competitors.

7   This company is planning to operate from fewer sites.

8   A rise in the value of this company's shares appears to depend on the success of its present strategy.

40

A

Angus
Since coming to the market five years ago, Angus has enjoyed great respect, considerably more than its peers in construction and building materials. This has been well deserved, with its initial profits now four times as great. However, the company's recent warning that such growth is unlikely to be maintained has caused a levelling off in its share price. Investors apparently want to see evidence that the current expansion into North America is paying off and paying for the large workforce, before pushing Angus shares any higher.

B

Johnson's
Steven Green, chairman of the ailing furniture manufacturer Johnson's, has produced his long-awaited turnaround plan for the company, comprising aggressive cost savings targets and some optimistic-looking profit forecasts. Further reducing the cost of raw materials by 15% is perhaps over-ambitious, given the resistance to the 5% cut the company imposed last year. Remaining savings should be more easily achievable through improving manufacturing efficiency, including job cuts and plant closures. Should Johnson's miss those targets, including returning to an operating profit as early as next year, Green's job could rapidly be in danger.

C

Hora Products
Four years ago, the shares of Hora Products, the watches and handbags distributor and retailer, stood at 405p. At that time, Hora revealed profits up by a third to £22m, but warned that growth was unlikely to continue at such a pace. The shares immediately dropped 11% and kept on falling, until they hit a trough of 64p. Last year Hora decided to concentrate on its volume divisions, which include the Lagoon and Horato watch brands, and disposed of all its luxury marques, a strategy that will be watched with interest by its rivals.

D

ForYou
A 2% drop in UK like-for-like sales in the last 3 months has forced healthcare retailers ForYou to issue a profit warning, with a suggestion that earnings for the year are likely to be cut by 10-15%. Management has been accused of over-optimism in believing it could deliver 40% new product growth annually. The turmoil resulting from this strategy will increase stock-carrying costs by £3m, and has resulted in the resignation of the director responsible for product and marketing. The shares closed on Friday at 76p, down 29% in the past year.

E

D&K
Consumer goods giant D&K has already abandoned the targets it set only six months ago. At the time, the new chief executive Gerald Lansbury made much of his move away from his predecessor's goals for growth in sales and earnings to more realistic figures. Clearly, though, his more modest ambitions are still not modest enough: D&K has real problems with losses in market share, and faces stagnating sales. Yesterday, sure enough, Lansbury set his sights even lower, blaming market conditions for the company's poor performance.

PART TWO

Questions 9–14

- Read this article about management buyouts.
- Choose the best sentence from the opposite page to fill each of the gaps.
- For each gap (**9–14**), mark one letter (**A–H**) on your Answer Sheet.
- Do not use any letter more than once.
- There is an example at the beginning (**0**).

How to launch a management buyout (MBO)

The business you're running has huge potential but the parent company doesn't seem interested, and there are rumours that they are looking to sell. If ever there's a time for you and your senior colleagues to mount a management buyout (that is, take over the company by purchasing its shares) it's now. (**0**) ..*H*.. That's why it's crucial to examine your motives carefully before doing anything.

According to Mark Perchetti, private equity partner at MYT Accountants, one motive for launching an MBO is to build some capital. (**9**) .... And this list is far from exhaustive. Before doing anything else, check the feasibility of a buyout. MBOs are invariably financed externally by borrowing money based on the company's share value (a leveraged buyout). That's why you will need to adopt strategies to sharply increase profits, by cutting costs or expanding, for example. This should enable you to significantly boost the value of the shares a few years down the line.

Approach the owners or parent company with your proposal and ask for permission before you disclose any confidential information to venture capitalists or banks. (**10**) .... And what you definitely don't want is to find yourself out of a job just yet!

So, when should you act? Well, it may be easier to raise the capital when business is booming, but paying over the odds is one of the biggest risks you face. (**11**) .... In other words, be careful not to pay too much. Also be careful who you choose for your team; this will typically consist of a CEO and 3-4 directors, but larger deals may bring in lower tiers. There's no room for sentiment. You may have someone who was fine as the accountant of an operating division, but who you then find is not up to being MD of an independent company. (**12**) .... To avoid this problem you should therefore consider bringing in external talent right from the start.

It's best to keep a low profile until your MBO is pretty much signed and sealed. (**13**) .... This might also mean that your customers, employees and other stakeholders become nervous, especially if there's a prolonged period of uncertainty. If there are key customers or suppliers whose ongoing commitment you require, wait until the last minute to talk to them. And remember, if your MBO fails, for whatever reason, you may find yourself working with the same colleagues and the current owners of the business. (**14**) .... So don't burn your bridges just yet!

Reading

Example: 0 | A B C D E F G **H**

A Other common reasons are where the business has become non-core to its parent, or where a private owner of a family business is retiring.

B If you are unfortunate enough to have to do this, they won't thank you if you have criticised their abilities or commitment.

C If you buy at the peak of the market, you may find it difficult ever to make money.

D Financiers want you to put in enough that it would hurt you if you lost it, but not so much that you'd be constantly worrying about it.

E If your financiers come to the same conclusion, you may lose credibility.

F If your interest becomes more widely known, you risk starting an auction, in which case the price will go up.

G Otherwise you risk being turned down at a later stage – and getting your marching orders.

H But the stakes are high: get it wrong and you could bankrupt yourself.

PART THREE

Questions 15–20

- Read the following article about the problems small companies may have in recruiting staff, and the questions on the opposite page.
- For each question (**15–20**), mark one letter (**A, B, C** or **D**) on your Answer Sheet.

Small companies often struggle in a crucial area – the recruitment of additional staff. With little time or budget for recruitment and training, mistakes are made all too easily.

Last year, Sally Thomas, managing director of a small software company, thought she had found the ideal project co-ordinator to handle long-term client relationships, after a two-year search. 'We had already tried a couple of internal people, but they were not suited to the role,' she says. 'The role does not require a detailed knowledge of information technology, but does demand enough expertise to understand current and future projects and the ability to talk about them meaningfully and sensitively to customers.' Ms Thomas and her technical director gave several short-listed candidates in-depth interviews and psychometric tests. They then decided to follow their instinct and pick the individual who had performed least well in the tests but felt like the right person for the job. The new project co-ordinator lasted just six weeks. 'It was very disappointing,' says Ms Thomas. 'In the end the psychometric test proved to be more accurate than our own belief in who was best.' Luckily the candidate who scored most highly in the tests was still available and is now doing well in the job.

Tony Jones used personal contacts when setting up his electronic repair services company, recruiting four people he already knew for the top management team. This worked well, but on technical staff he has been less successful, with a 50% drop-out rate in just four months. 'It's easy to make snap judgements because you're so busy running the business,' Mr Jones says. 'Instead of a thorough testing process you tend to do it too fast. Someone seems like a nice person who knows what they're doing, so you give them the job but eventually you come to regret your decision.'

Mr Jones has tried employment agencies, but finds them expensive and lacking in knowledge of sectors such as electronics. 'Finding electronic engineers is not like looking for bankers for example,' he says. 'The right people for us tend to have been stuck in the bedroom with a soldering iron in their youth, rather than having done particularly well academically. We could be talking about the dark side of the moon as far as most agencies are concerned.'

Recruitment from outside is a huge problem for small companies, but according to Louise Punter, chief executive of the Surrey Chamber of Commerce, 'People who have moved from other firms bring a fresh look and a big injection of new ideas.' Those who have worked for medium-sized or large companies are particularly valuable, because they are familiar with processes and systems that can be just as effective in a company of ten people as in a company of thousands. 'Small companies tend to deal only with the immediate problem, whereas a larger organisation would put in place a process that would prevent the same thing going wrong again. People who know how to do this can be very valuable.'

On the other hand, given the current skills shortage, low unemployment and the expense involved in recruitment, it makes sense to promote from within where possible. 'A classic mistake is that companies overlook the skills their existing staff have; for example, a marketing person might have good financial skills,' says Mrs Punter. She recommends conducting a skills audit to identify staff expertise, in particular what is transferable or not being fully exploited. In larger companies, these issues often come out in appraisals, but in small ones they are easily missed.

Not surprisingly, finding the right staff can present small companies with their biggest challenge.

15 Appointing a new project co-ordinator made Sally Thomas realise that

   A   she had misjudged the value of different methods of selection.
   B   few people had the right combination of qualities for the job.
   C   she had underestimated the time required to choose the best candidate.
   D   internal promotion was unlikely to lead to a successful appointment.

16 In the third paragraph, what point does Tony Jones make?

   A   Different jobs require candidates to have different qualities.
   B   The demands of running a business ought to take priority over interviewing.
   C   The most effective method of selection is personal contact.
   D   A mistake in the choice of candidate can have a long-term effect.

17 What criticism does Tony Jones make of agencies?

   A   They do not hold enough discussions with employers.
   B   They fail to focus on the appropriate skills.
   C   They underestimate the demand for electronic engineers.
   D   They do not react quickly enough to technical developments.

18 According to Louise Punter, it is useful for small companies to recruit people who

   A   understand the problems of small businesses.
   B   have experience of similar-sized organisations.
   C   can apply knowledge gained elsewhere.
   D   have designed systems in their previous job.

19 In the sixth paragraph, what point does Louise Punter make about small companies?

   A   They are not likely to be able to afford to recruit staff with the right skills.
   B   They lack the necessary skills for carrying out staff appraisals.
   C   They may not be aware of some of the skills of their employees.
   D   They depend too heavily on staff developing appropriate marketing skills.

20 Which of the following is the writer's main point in the article as a whole?

   A   Finding the right people is crucial for small companies.
   B   Many of the selection tools used by large companies are unsuitable for small companies.
   C   Recruitment experts should provide a better service for small companies.
   D   Small companies need to reduce the cost of recruiting new staff.

Test 2

PART FOUR

Questions 21–30

- Read the extract below from a bank's advice to businesses about finding and keeping customers.
- Choose the correct word to fill each gap from **A**, **B**, **C** or **D** on the opposite page.
- For each question (**21–30**), mark one letter (**A**, **B**, **C** or **D**) on your Answer Sheet.
- There is an example at the beginning (**0**).

Finding and keeping customers

Customers and buyers are the lifeblood of any business. The constant challenge is to first find your customers and then sell to them.

For businesses which are just (**0**) .... up, marketing professionals suggest working out a SWOT analysis – a systematic review of your Strengths, Weaknesses, Opportunities and Threats – to clarify your business thinking and (**21**) .... realistic sales targets.

Once you've gained customers it's important to remember that they can (**22**) .... or break your business. After all, if you give excellent service, they will freely advertise your company to colleagues and friends, giving you a competitive (**23**) .... over your rivals.

When you're planning to pay for advertising, business directories, local newspapers and the internet can be very cost-effective. Trade exhibitions can also (**24**) .... you to a wide range of useful contacts and lucrative new markets.

You may also be able to (**25**) .... company news into free PR by sending press (**26**) .... to magazines and newspapers. But editors have very (**27**) .... space, so your story must be unusually interesting and entertaining to (**28**) .... in print.

At JS Bank we specialise in helping new businesses (**29**) .... off to a promising start. We can help you develop your business, and our free book *How to (**30**) .... your business potential* is a detailed, practical guide to advertising, endorsed by the Institute of Direct Marketing. Contact your local JS Bank for a copy.

Example:

A starting   B coming   C growing   D bringing

| 0 | A ■ | B ☐ | C ☐ | D ☐ |

21	A form	B place	C set	D shape
22	A do	B make	C take	D put
23	A benefit	B bonus	C margin	D edge
24	A introduce	B initiate	C encounter	D present
25	A direct	B turn	C point	D steer
26	A leaflets	B campaigns	C shots	D releases
27	A short	B small	C limited	D lacking
28	A appear	B display	C show	D represent
29	A stand	B get	C go	D move
30	A advantage	B practise	C employ	D exploit

PART FIVE

Questions 31–40

- Read the article below about a manufacturing company.
- For each question (**31–40**), write one word in CAPITAL LETTERS on your Answer Sheet.
- There is an example at the beginning (**0**).

Example: | 0 | S | U | C | H | | | | |

Company focus – PWT

Within the Telcar group, PWT, maker of energy management systems, is a small player and as (**0**) .... has little influence over broad group strategic direction and resource allocation. (**31**) .... this, the company can point to a history of operational excellence on (**32**) .... it has built up a 30% market share under the nose of competitor Blacktons.

Success has been hard won. Before 1990, the main plant, which accounts (**33**) .... three-quarters of company turnover, made its products in traditional mass-production push-mode – building batches for stock to complex schedules and forecasts. Lead times were long, even (**34**) .... the warehouse was always bulging with stock, and customer satisfaction was low.

A substantial loss in 1995 finally resulted in PWT making fundamental changes in order to survive. Taking a collective deep breath, it moved to stockless production using JIT (just-in-time) principles and production cells in place of the previous assembly line. (**35**) .... sooner had it done so than it began to see dramatic results, e.g. lead times slashed from six weeks to three days. Without forecasting and scheduling, materials control became massively simplified.

(**36**) .... really enabled PWT to compete (**37**) .... equal terms anywhere in the world were its unbeatable lead times and consistent quality. So efficient had the company's practices become (**38**) .... in 2004 it moved production to a new site with no downtime, meaning that (**39**) .... even a single order was missed.

The next phase? The company is now engaged (**40**) .... introducing a redesigned range. In the group context, it's as a centre of manufacturing excellence that PWT can keep on punching above its weight.

PART SIX

Questions 41–52

- Read the text below about teamworking.
- In most of the lines (**41–52**), there is one extra word. It is either grammatically incorrect or does not fit in with the meaning of the text. Some lines, however, are correct.
- If a line is correct, write **CORRECT** on your Answer Sheet.
- If there is an extra word in the line, write **the extra word** in CAPITAL LETTERS on your Answer Sheet.
- The exercise begins with two examples (**0** and **00**).

Examples:

0	O	F				

00	C	O	R	R	E	C	T

Supporting the weakest link in your team

0   A good, well-balanced work team is like a family in the sense that of its

00 individual members couldn't manage without each other. As long as each

41 person does what is expected of them and plays their part to the best way of

42 their ability, and the cogs keep turning smoothly. Everyone has off-days,

43 when the simplest tasks seem impossible, you can't concentrate on or be

44 bothered. But it's when a colleague's some off-days turn into off-weeks, then

45 off-months, that warning bells will start to sound. High-performance teams

46 have clear standards of what there is acceptable behaviour. If the rest of

47 the team perceives so that one person isn't pulling their weight or is being

48 incompetent, it affects everyone. You should need to find out the reason for

49 your colleague's exact non-performance. If someone has suddenly stopped

50 performing, become withdrawn or is lacking in motivation, it could be due to a

51 personal problem. Then again, as their ineptitude could be down to lack of

52 experience or confidence. Encourage them to take up full advantage of

    training and other schemes designed to help them.

Test 2

WRITING 1 hour 10 minutes

PART ONE

Question 1

- The graph below shows the number of permanent full-time, permanent part-time and temporary contract employees in a software design company called Radnor Design over a four-year period.
- Using the information from the graph, write a short **report** comparing the number of full-time employees with the number of part-time and contract employees.
- Write **120–140** words.

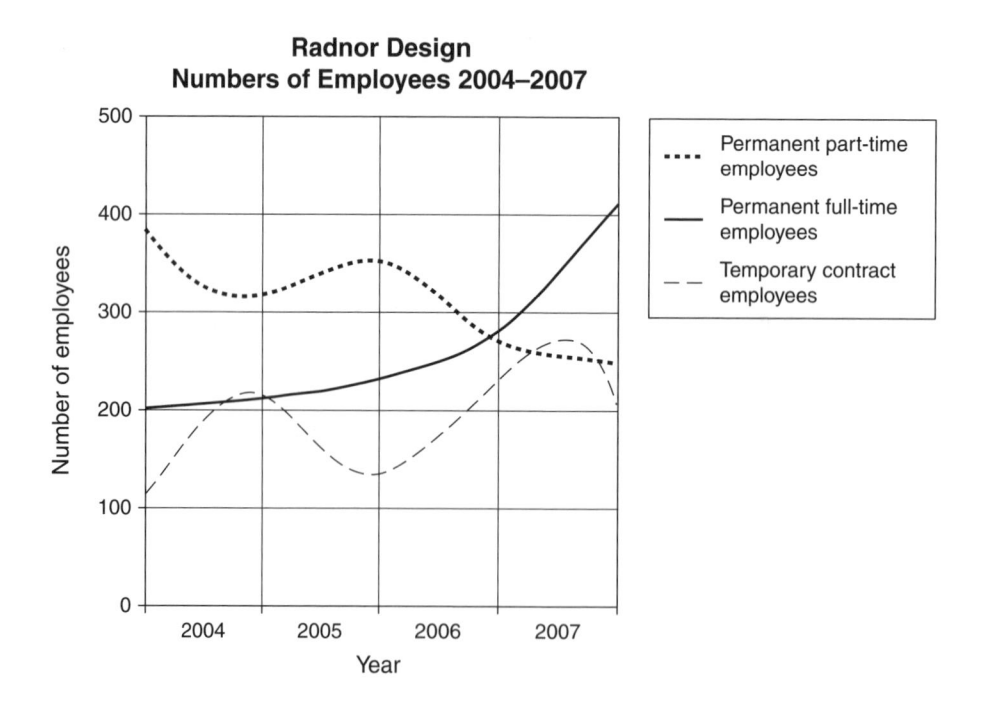

**Radnor Design
Numbers of Employees 2004–2007**

- - - - Permanent part-time employees
——— Permanent full-time employees
– – Temporary contract employees

PART TWO

Write an answer to **one** of the questions **2–4** in this part. Write your answer in **200–250** words.

Question 2

- You work in your company's head office and you have recently visited one of the company's retail outlets. Your line manager has asked you to write a report on your visit.
- Write the **report** for your line manager, including the following information:
  - a brief description of the store you visited
  - an assessment of the performance and attitude of the staff
  - a suggestion for improving the store.

Question 3

- Your company uses an external transport company to distribute its products. However, there have recently been some problems, and you are considering changing to another company. Your boss has asked you to contact a possible new distribution company.
- Write a **letter** to the distribution company:
  - outlining what your company does
  - describing your transport requirements
  - explaining how you expect your transport requirements to change in the next few years
  - giving details of the information you would like to receive from the distribution company.

Question 4

- The management board of your company is considering closing its three small offices in the city centre and relocating to different premises outside the city. You have been asked to submit a proposal to the board concerning the possible relocation.
- Write your **proposal** for the board:
  - explaining why you think the company needs to relocate
  - giving a brief description of the type of premises that will be required
  - assessing the possible impact of the move on staff
  - assessing the possible impact of the move on the company's business.

Test 2

LISTENING   Approximately 40 minutes (including 10 minutes' transfer time)

PART ONE

Questions 1–12

- You will hear a representative of SGC, a telecoms company, giving a talk to a group of business students about SGC.
- As you listen, for questions **1–12**, complete the notes using up to three words or a number.
- After you have listened once, replay the recording.

SGC

SGC's strengths

1   strong .... identity in all current markets

2   particular focus on .... market

3   high-quality .... resulting from investment

4   new package of .... maintains satisfaction

5   high level of .... leading to innovation

SGC's strategic initiatives for the future

6   to start promoting image of being .... and ....

7   to start using new forms of .... in attractive formats

8   to reduce .... by 25%

9   to increase income from .... revenues

10 to establish several ....

Market opportunities

11 service providers moving to .... products

12 high .... leading to increased revenues

52

PART TWO

Questions 13–22

- You will hear five people talking about workshops they have recently attended.
- For each extract, there are two tasks. For Task One, choose the reason the speaker gives for attending the workshop from the list **A–H**. For Task Two, choose the outcome of attending the workshop from the list **A–H**.
- After you have listened once, replay the recording.

Task One – Reason for choosing to attend

- For questions **13–17**, match the extracts with the reason for attending the workshop, listed **A–H**.
- For each extract, choose the reason for attending the workshop that each person mentions.
- Write one letter (**A–H**) next to the number of the extract.

13	Speaker 1	A	to learn how to achieve innovation
		B	to widen network of contacts
14	Speaker 2	C	to deepen understanding of theory
15	Speaker 3	D	to increase effectiveness in research
		E	to manage information more effectively
16	Speaker 4	F	to explore issues in managing recruitment
		G	to consider methods of performance appraisal
17	Speaker 5	H	to examine evidence of changing trends

Task Two – Outcome of attending

- For questions **18–22**, match the extracts with the outcome of attending the workshop, listed **A–H**.
- For each extract, choose the outcome of attending the workshop that each person mentions.
- Write one letter (**A–H**) next to the number of the extract.

18	Speaker 1	A	A report was produced for senior staff.
		B	Job specifications were revised.
19	Speaker 2	C	A project team was established.
20	Speaker 3	D	Information was made available to all staff.
		E	Achievement targets were introduced.
21	Speaker 4	F	Outside advice was sought.
		G	A new position was created.
22	Speaker 5	H	An external survey was commissioned.

Test 2

PART THREE

Questions 23–30

- You will hear a discussion between two business journalists, Nick and Rachel, who are going to write a review of a book about career planning.
- For each question (**23–30**), mark one letter (**A**, **B** or **C**) for the correct answer.
- After you have listened once, replay the recording.

23 What does Nick say about the title of the book?

    A It suggests a serious approach to career planning.
    B It gives a false impression about the content of the book.
    C It is reminiscent of books previously published on this subject.

24 What did Rachel find disappointing about the advice given in the book?

    A It tended to state the obvious.
    B It was often irrelevant to her.
    C It seemed to lack authority.

25 According to Nick, the author's previous books

    A suggest she has little direct experience of business.
    B demonstrate a failure to reflect current business practice.
    C highlight an absence of original research in her work.

26 Rachel particularly enjoyed reading the section on

    A going for job interviews.
    B consulting career advisors.
    C completing job applications.

27 Both journalists agree that a major weakness of the book is that

    A it is aimed at those who are already established in their careers.
    B it focuses on a kind of career path that has become less common.
    C it relies too much on experiences of people at the end of their careers.

28 Rachel disagrees with the book's suggestion that readers should

    A keep changing jobs in order to achieve career success.
    B choose a field that matches their leisure activities.
    C take a particular test to identify a suitable career.

29 What does Rachel think about the cost of the book?

    A   It would be beyond the budget of any business student.
    B   It will discourage readers looking for an academic text.
    C   It compares favourably to other books of this kind.

30 Nick anticipates that people who buy the book will

    A   read the whole text in one go.
    B   read one chapter at a time.
    C   read only the case studies.

You now have 10 minutes to transfer your answers to your Answer Sheet.

Test 2

SPEAKING   16 minutes

SAMPLE SPEAKING TASKS

PART ONE

In this part, the interlocutor asks questions to each of the candidates in turn. You have to give information about yourself and express personal opinions.

PART TWO

In this part of the test, you are asked to give a short talk on a business topic. You have to choose one of the topics from the three below and then talk for about one minute. You have one minute to prepare your ideas.

> A **Career development:** the importance of being willing to make long business trips
>
> B **Purchasing:** how to ensure that a company's suppliers consistently meet delivery deadlines
>
> C **Corporate culture:** the importance of all staff understanding the corporate culture of their company

PART THREE

In this part of the test, you are given a discussion topic. You have 30 seconds to look at the task prompt, an example of which is below, and then about three minutes to discuss the topic with your partner. After that, the examiner will ask you more questions related to the topic.

For **two** candidates

> ### Travelling to Work
>
> Your company's location in a busy city centre means that staff often complain about the time taken to get to work. You have been asked to make some recommendations.
>
> Discuss and decide together:
>
> - whether it would be better for staff to use public or private transport
> - what the effects might be of allowing staff to work flexible hours.

For **three** candidates

Travelling to Work

Your company's location in a busy city centre means that staff often complain about the time taken to get to work. You have been asked to make some recommendations.

Discuss and decide together:

- whether it would be better for staff to use public or private transport
- what the effects might be of allowing staff to work flexible hours
- what other measures the company could take to deal with the situation.

Follow-on questions

- Would you be willing to spend a long time travelling to work every day? (Why?/Why not?)

- Should companies provide staff with financial assistance if they have long journeys to work? (Why?/Why not?)

- What do you think influences a company's decision to be located in a busy city centre? (Why?)

- What effect do you think technology will have in the future on where people do their work? (Why?)

- What could be the long-term effect of changes in the hours people work and where they work? (Why?)

Test 3

READING 1 hour

PART ONE

Questions 1–8

- Look at the statements below and the five extracts from an article about 'offshoring', the shift of service jobs to other countries, on the opposite page.
- Which extract (**A, B, C, D** or **E**) does each statement (**1–8**) refer to?
- For each statement (**1–8**), mark one letter (**A, B, C, D** or **E**) on your Answer Sheet.
- You will need to use some of these letters more than once.
- There is an example at the beginning (**0**).

Example:

0 Offshore functions will not necessarily stay abroad as financial considerations change.

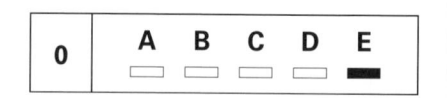

0 A B C D **E**

1   There is evidence that the use of offshoring will increase.

2   Offshoring is not an option in certain sectors.

3   The structure of businesses can make offshoring problematic.

4   People consulting offshore staff may find the service unsatisfactory.

5   Offshoring is still an untried and untested concept for many companies.

6   Technology may enable companies to target aspects of their business for offshoring.

7   The benefits of offshoring are not confined to lower costs.

8   Strategic planning in the location of services may facilitate more successful offshoring.

Offshoring

A

An article in *McKinsey Quarterly* says that some companies which have moved their back-office functions offshore have missed huge opportunities to reap efficiencies beyond those that come from just using cheaper labour. These companies often merely replicate what they do at home, where labour is expensive and capital is relatively cheap, in countries in which the reverse is true. They forget an additional benefit is that offshoring allows companies to work round-the-clock shifts, ferrying data back and forth from one place to another, and that it also allows them to rethink the way they solve IT problems. The most successful operators redesign business processes to take full advantage of the new environment's potential.

B

There is no doubt that customers with complex queries requiring local understanding do not respond well to far-off operators repeating a series of specially learned responses. Convergys, one of the world's biggest providers of 'contact-centre services', advises companies to shift simple queries offshore while retaining the more complex ones on the same shore as the caller. It calls this process 'rightshoring', and estimates that about 80% of the companies that it is working with in Britain are planning to split their call-centre operations in this way.

C

Harris Miller, president of the Information Technology Association of America, a lobby group, says that offshore locations have so far captured just 3–4% of all American companies' outsourcing. The bulk remains onshore in the hands of big firms such as Accenture and IBM. In fact, 60% of major corporates are doing nothing, or are only just beginning to investigate the potential of offshoring. Nevertheless, some big companies have told him that up to 40% of their outsourced business could end up offshore. That suggests the industry still has a long way to grow.

D

One thing currently limiting the ability of companies to outsource tasks offshore is the inflexible architecture of modern business-information systems. It forces firms to perform tasks as a series of discrete steps. So a business wanting to outsource some of those steps (billing, for instance), but not others, gets involved in complicated flows of information that are prone to error. Newer software and hardware promise a future in which firms will be able to outsource smaller slivers of their business. They will not, as now, have to commit to outsourcing the whole of a department or nothing.

E

Many service jobs are in industries like hotels and restaurants, or in public services like education and health, most of which can never be moved abroad. There are also alternative pools of labour to be tapped at home. Citigroup, for instance, has hired about 100 college students in America to do programming for it. In addition, some of the tasks currently going to low-cost offshore centres may eventually return because their underlying technologies will evolve in such a way that it makes economic sense to put them back in the home country.

PART TWO

Questions 9–14

- Read this text about the growing demand for consultants, taken from a business magazine.
- Choose the best sentence from the opposite page to fill each of the gaps.
- For each gap (**9–14**), mark one letter (**A–H**) on your Answer Sheet.
- Do not use any letter more than once.
- There is an example at the beginning (**0**).

EVERYBODY WANTS CONSULTANTS

Management consultancy firms have always found it easy to lure business school graduates, with the students themselves rating the sector top of their wish list. (**0**) ...*H*... It is this obstacle to successful growth that consultancies are seeking to overcome.

One of the main attractions of consultancy has always been the high level of starting salaries. (**9**) .... In industrial companies, pay rises usually come in steps and are wide apart, while consultants' pay tends to increase constantly and follow a steeper curve. Consultants also appreciate their autonomy, and the opportunity to broaden their experience, acquiring competences in several sectors.

The rewards of the job are more tangible than those for managers employed by companies. Consultants enjoy predicting the changes that their recommendations will make. (**10**) .... In fact, such factors mean some consultants play down the importance of pay as a motivating factor. (**11**) .... For example, consultants may be working in teams where as many as ten different nationalities are represented.

Despite all this, moves out of consultancy into the corporate world are more common than the other way round. (**12**) .... As a result of such ambition, retaining talented staff is a constant challenge for consultancy firms. In this respect, they are sometimes victims of their own strengths, having drawn in recruits with promises that after two years in consultancy young graduates will be able to do almost any job. (**13**) .... The temptation is worrying for consultancy firms as demand for their services, and so their people, continues to grow at a prodigious rate, creating a huge recruitment need. (**14**) .... But so far, consultants recruited from the outside, as opposed to fresh from business schools, who adapt successfully remain a minority. This is largely due to the strong corporate cultures they have been part of.

It will be interesting to see how the situation develops over the next few years. Whatever happens, it is clear that there will be plenty of demand for consultants.

Example:

0	A B C D E F G H

A It feels even better if they are still around when these are implemented.

B They claim rather that they benefit from the whole working style, partly due to the degree of diversity within the job.

C These also then grow faster than in other sectors, according to frequently published comparisons.

D But people in industry also consider such adaptability valuable and make very attractive offers to consultants, which are hard to resist.

E It leaves them no choice but to develop the ability to integrate managers switching from industry.

F The growing trend of hiring consultants from companies owes much to the shortage of qualifying graduates.

G It is a path which is particularly visible among new graduates, who tend to view consultancy as a stepping stone towards a managerial position.

H What has been proving more difficult is appealing to people who already occupy managerial positions within companies.

PART THREE

Questions 15–20

- Read the following article about a US manufacturer of office supplies and the questions on the opposite page.
- For each question (**15–20**), mark one letter (**A, B, C** or **D**) on your Answer Sheet.

In 1761 the German cabinet-maker Caspar Faber started a small business producing pencils. Three generations later, in the nineteenth century, the firm was run by Lothar von Faber, whose innovations included a hexagonal pencil to prevent it from rolling, and a system to designate the hardness of lead, which was eventually adopted by other manufacturers in the industry. Exports to the USA began in 1843, with a New York subsidiary set up six years later to handle the US end of the business, under the management of Lothar's brother Eberhard. This firm subsequently started making its own pencils, using leads imported from its German parent company, until in 1903 the two companies separated. Eberhard Faber, the US company, became a competitor of the German business, now called Faber-Castell.

By the 1970s, Eberhard Faber, originator of the yellow pencil familiar to generations of North Americans, had a 10% share of the $100 million pencil market. The company's sales of pencils, pens, erasers, and rubber bands were increasing in developing countries, but recent US sales were essentially static. As a result, Eberhard Faber's US pencil sales accounted for less than 20% of its worldwide sales, and by the end of the decade the company's total US earnings had declined.

The pencil market became particularly competitive in the early 1980s, and Eberhard Faber's top management concluded that the key to greater US profitability was marketing. At first the firm made some mistakes. For example, after producing yellow pencils for nearly a century, the company decided to introduce a natural-looking pencil: bare cedar wood covered with a coat of clear lacquer. Eberhard Faber projected a 15% market share for the new product, thinking that the current trend toward naturalness would carry over into the pencil market. But stationers avoided the new product, preferring to stick with a proven seller.

Another strategic miscalculation involved the company's redoubled efforts in art supplies, a market that yields greater profit margins than the highly competitive office supplies market. Because Eberhard Faber's design markers were already successful, the company acquired several art supply firms. At the same time, however, it began to put less emphasis in the commercial office supplies field that accounted for two-thirds of its total sales. In this market, which included sales to corporations under own-brand labels as well as the Eberhard Faber name, the firm found itself gaining a reputation for non-competitive pricing and sluggish new-product development, despite the consistently good quality and service it actually offered.

Later in the 1980s new executives tried to revamp every aspect of the company's ineffective marketing operation. They also developed new products, such as five-sided erasers in stylish colours. Nearly every product package was updated. Such moves benefited the company's image, but despite its efforts Eberhard Faber was still struggling, and began seeking a buyer. Faber-Castell, seeing an opportunity to increase market share and protect the Faber trade name, made the landmark acquisition of Eberhard Faber in 1987, reuniting the two firms. After further major changes, in 1996 a new Faber-Castell was once again established as a wholly-owned US company.

The new Faber-Castell USA concentrated on high end markets, and soon launched an exclusive collection of premium writing instruments and accessories, intended to bring back the handwriting culture that had been thrown aside by modern technology. According to Till Quante, the company's marketing manager for fine writing instruments, when the calculator and later the personal computer were introduced, those in love with technology predicted the pencil companies would die, but, 'Just the opposite happened,' says Quante. Faber-Castell is confident of a bright future.

15 The US company run by Eberhard Faber was set up in order to

   A trade in pencils from a variety of sources.
   B manufacture pencils using imported leads.
   C compete with German pencil manufacturers.
   D find customers for its parent company's products.

16 What are we told about Eberhard Faber's situation in the 1970s?

   A Sales in one of its markets were not matching rises elsewhere.
   B Its main product line was generating a declining share of its income.
   C Attempts to diversify into new products were proving unsuccessful.
   D It was losing market share to a number of competitors.

17 What problem did Eberhard Faber face when it introduced cedar wood pencils?

   A Customers demanded the reintroduction of yellow pencils.
   B Stockists felt it was too risky to try to sell them.
   C Consumers objected to the materials that were used.
   D Marketing of the products proved too expensive.

18 According to the fourth paragraph, what strategic mistake did Eberhard Faber make?

   A It moved into a market with which it was unfamiliar.
   B It allowed the quality of its products to fall.
   C It neglected volume sales in favour of profit margins.
   D It concentrated on selling products to be sold under own-brand labels.

19 According to the fifth paragraph, in the 1980s Eberhard Faber was failing to

   A achieve financial security.
   B retain its senior managers.
   C improve its public image.
   D revise its product range.

20 According to the last paragraph, Faber-Castell USA is implementing a strategy of

   A reviving traditional forms of advertising.
   B targeting a specific type of customer.
   C using technology in product development.
   D relaunching previously discontinued products.

PART FOUR

Questions 21–30

- Read the article below about an attempt to buy part of a company.
- Choose the correct word to fill each gap from **A**, **B**, **C** or **D** on the opposite page.
- For each question (**21–30**), mark one letter (**A**, **B**, **C** or **D**) on your Answer Sheet.
- There is an example at the beginning (**0**).

DATA INTERNATIONAL TO KEEP WAVERTREE

Data International, the heavily indebted book and music retailer, has shelved plans to sell its Wavertree book (**0**) .... to Morris Media, after the two sides failed to come to an agreement on a price. Morris Media, which had been negotiating with Wavertree for over a year, had come forward with a (**21**) .... of close to £200 million for the business. Data International is thought to have wanted closer to £300 million. Disagreement arose over the level of working (**22**) .... in the business, coupled with problems of the rising cost of bank debt needed to help (**23**) .... the purchase.

It is believed that the directors of Data International backed away from the sale as Wavertree's (**24**) .... had begun to improve. Last year Wavertree (**25**) .... profits of around £30 million before interest, tax and depreciation, on sales of around £400 million. Some observers believe that Data International is playing for time in the hope that Wavertree will (**26**) .... from a hefty increase in sales in the key end-of-year period which may help (**27**) .... the price that the company can ask for Wavertree if talks resume some time in the new year.

A representative of Data International said, 'Sales at our music stores increased by 6% in the first quarter of the current financial year while Wavertree saw an increase of 9.5% over the same period. The company remains (**28**) .... to Wavertree and the vote taken by the board to (**29**) .... Wavertree for the foreseeable future was (**30**) ....'

64

Example:

	A	wing	B	chain	C	market	D	section

0	A ☐ B ■ C ☐ D ☐

21	A	contract	B	deal	C	pledge	D	bid
22	A	capital	B	assets	C	investments	D	cash
23	A	fund	B	pay	C	acquire	D	buy
24	A	behaviour	B	functions	C	performance	D	transactions
25	A	established	B	gained	C	brought	D	generated
26	A	promote	B	benefit	C	assist	D	favour
27	A	enlarge	B	swell	C	boost	D	advance
28	A	devoted	B	guaranteed	C	associated	D	committed
29	A	possess	B	retain	C	carry	D	proceed
30	A	unanimous	B	total	C	unified	D	complete

PART FIVE

Questions 31–40

- Read the article below about collaborating at work.
- For each question (**31–40**), write one word in CAPITAL LETTERS on your Answer Sheet.
- There is an example at the beginning (**0**).

Example: `0` `D` `O`

Successful collaboration

When colleagues act in ways that seem unproductive, they are likely to (**0**) .... so for a reason. Few people have the goal of preventing you from getting things done. (**31**) .... is more likely that they are responding rationally to a perceived interest. Someone may be abrupt because he is faced (**32**) .... an important deadline and wants to get back to work. Another may disparage an attempt to be creative because she has high standards, and wants to keep looking for an even better idea. (**33**) .... there might be more constructive ways for them to pursue such goals, these goals are usually legitimate. Try to imagine (**34**) .... the motivation for their behaviour might be. When you discuss an issue with colleagues, start with the assumption that they would (**35**) .... prepared to help. 'I know you have been terribly busy and perhaps concerned about cutting costs. Still I would welcome your thinking about an issue that is on (**36**) .... mind.'

Knowing that you want to see their point of view will make it easier (**37**) .... them to see yours. And it will reassure them that you appreciate their concerns, and that any new proposal will (**38**) .... those concerns into account. The degree of successful collaboration in a group is the sum of individual behaviour. Everyone contributes (**39**) .... the difficulties. *You* may not be aware of the extent to (**40**) .... you affect the dynamics of the group, but your colleagues almost certainly are.

PART SIX

Questions 41–52

- Read the text below about changes in employment patterns in the UK.
- In most of the lines (**41–52**), there is one extra word. It is either grammatically incorrect or does not fit in with the meaning of the text. Some lines, however, are correct.
- If a line is correct, write **CORRECT** on your Answer Sheet.
- If there is an extra word in the line, write **the extra word** in CAPITAL LETTERS on your Answer Sheet.
- The exercise begins with two examples (**0** and **00**).

Examples:

| 0 | T | H | E | I | R | | |
| 00 | C | O | R | R | E | C | T |

The changing nature of employment in the UK

0	The unwritten contract between worker and their employer is changing rapidly. No
00	longer is an employer able to guarantee anybody a job, or even a career, for
41	the life. Neither should employees attempt to wed themselves to an
42	organisation for the promise of security, such as it will not be there. If we, as
43	employees, are to survive, then we will have to make the effort to change too. It
44	is simply no longer well enough to sit tight in our office chairs and hope that
45	somehow, if we keep quiet, we will be overlooked but when the hammer of
46	redundancy strikes. It will be the survival of the fittest and there will be few
47	exceptions. The rules have changed too. Qualifications all alone will no longer
48	guarantee promotion as they might have done this in the past. In these new
49	circumstances, employees will be judged on their ability how to resolve conflict,
50	negotiate a solid contract, motivate people under them to work so hard, and
51	demonstrate a considerable amount of personal commitment towards their future of
52	development. It is certainly going to be tough to get ahead and, as if for staying
	ahead, that will be tougher still.

Test 3

WRITING   1 hour 10 minutes

PART ONE

Question 1

- The bar chart below shows the average numbers of conference attendees in three categories at three different conferences organised by the Central Business Centre.
- Using the information from the chart, write a short **report** describing and comparing the attendance patterns at the conferences.
- Write **120–140** words.

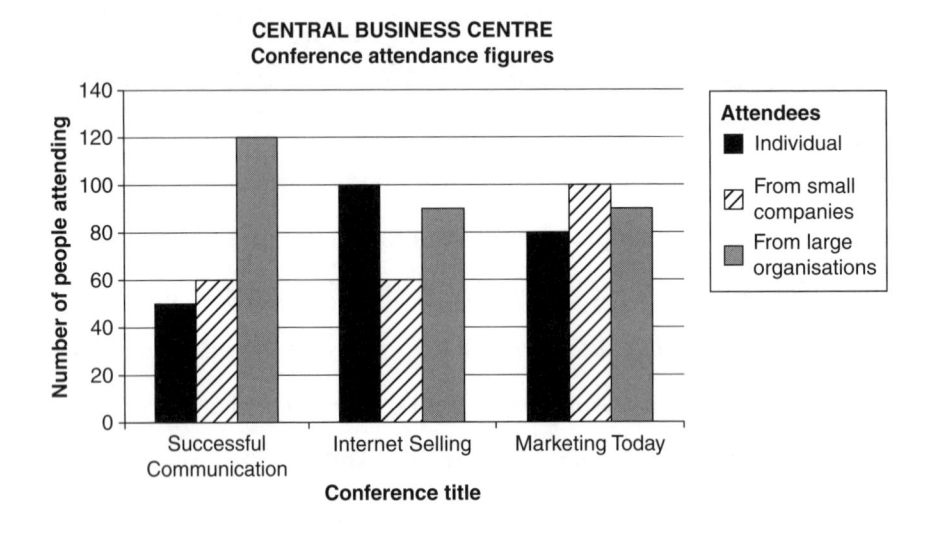

CENTRAL BUSINESS CENTRE
Conference attendance figures

Attendees:
- Individual
- From small companies
- From large organisations

Successful Communication: Individual 50, From small companies 60, From large organisations 120
Internet Selling: Individual 100, From small companies 60, From large organisations 90
Marketing Today: Individual 80, From small companies 100, From large organisations 90

Y-axis: Number of people attending (0–140)
X-axis: Conference title

68

Writing

PART TWO

Write an answer to **one** of the questions **2–4** in this part. Write your answer in **200-250** words.

Question 2

- One of your biggest customers recently started purchasing from a competitor instead of from your organisation, and your Managing Director has asked you to investigate the reasons for this.
- Write your **report** for the Managing Director:
  - explaining how you investigated the reasons
  - giving details of what you discovered
  - suggesting a way of dealing with the situation.

Question 3

- An international business magazine recently published an article about your company. However, the article contained a number of errors and was quite negative about your company, so your line manager has asked you to write to the editor of the magazine.
- Write a **letter** to the editor of the magazine:
  - describing the errors that the article contained
  - presenting a detailed defence of the company
  - suggesting what you would like the editor to do.

Question 4

- Your company's sales have been falling significantly. The Managing Director believes that the current marketing strategy is inadequate and needs revising. You have been asked to write a proposal for a new marketing strategy.
- Write your **proposal** for the Managing Director:
  - explaining what is wrong with the current marketing strategy
  - outlining some ideas for a new marketing strategy
  - giving reasons why these ideas would be effective.

Test 3

LISTENING   Approximately 40 minutes (including 10 minutes' transfer time)

PART ONE

Questions 1–12

- You will hear a recording that a training manager has made for his assistant, describing plans for a training day that he will be running with his colleague, Julia.
- As you listen, for questions **1–12**, complete the notes using up to three words or a number.
- After you have listened once, replay the recording.

TRAINING DAY FOR STANDFORD'S

THINGS TO DO

Ring Swan Hotel, request (**1**) .... (in addition to other equipment booked).

Cancel (**2**) ....

Remind participants to bring the (**3**) .... they've received to the training day.

Tell Standford's that the title of the talk by the guest speaker is now (**4**) '...........................'.

PROGRAMME

Morning

9.15: Talk on: The value of (**5**) .... in business

10.00: Workshop: (**6**) ....

11.15: Discussion: (**7**) '...........................'

12.00: Role play: (**8**) ....

1.00: Lunch

Afternoon

2.00: Session: (**9**) ....

3.15: Either

     Presentation: (**10**) '...........................'

     or

     Workshop: (**11**) '...........................'

4.00: (**12**) ....

5.00: Finish

PART TWO

Questions 13–22

- You will hear five different people talking about the issues involved in having new buildings constructed and advice about new construction projects.
- For each extract, there are two tasks. For Task One, decide what problem occurred with the construction project from the list **A–H**. For Task Two, choose what advice about new construction projects each speaker gives from the list **A–H**.
- After you have listened once, replay the recording.

Task One – Problem with new construction project

- For questions **13–17**, match the extracts with the problem that occurred with the new construction project, listed **A–H**.
- For each extract, choose the problem that occurred with the new construction project.
- Write one letter (**A–H**) next to the number of the extract.

13	Speaker 1	A	A completion stage on the building was missed.
		B	Spending on installations exceeded projected figures.
14	Speaker 2	C	The managers' offices were poorly located.
15	Speaker 3	D	Equipment was inadequately tested.
		E	Ineffective air-conditioning was installed.
16	Speaker 4	F	Insufficient parking space was provided for delivery vehicles.
17	Speaker 5	G	Plans failed to include access to the site.
		H	Contractors' costs went over budget.

Task Two – Advice about new construction projects

- For questions **18–22**, match the extracts with the advice about new construction projects, listed **A–H**.
- For each extract, choose the advice about new construction projects.
- Write one letter (**A–H**) next to the number of the extract.

18	Speaker 1	A	Use an external company to research the site.
		B	Negotiate good deals for servicing agreements.
19	Speaker 2	C	Invite firms to tender for parts of the project.
20	Speaker 3	D	Set up a special team to manage the expansion.
		E	Investigate alternative methods of expansion.
21	Speaker 4	F	Consult senior staff on details.
		G	Only use reputable contractors.
22	Speaker 5	H	Set stages of completion for different parts.

Test 3

PART THREE

Questions 23–30

- You will hear a meeting involving members of a quality improvement group in a manufacturing company. The department head, Sandra, is talking to a female colleague, Fiona, and a male colleague, Jamie.
- For each question (**23–30**), mark one letter (**A**, **B** or **C**) for the correct answer.
- After you have listened once, replay the recording.

23 The group's agreed solution to the telephone problem is designed to stop

    A callers complaining about being kept waiting.
    B staff refusing to answer other people's phones.
    C calls coming through to someone who cannot help.

24 Concerning telephone answering times, the group agrees to

    A carry out research into the current situation.
    B provide staff training in telephone skills.
    C set measurable standards for answering.

25 The man suggests using the internet to

    A advertise the company's products.
    B find out about the competition.
    C search for potential customers.

26 What does the group agree to recommend as a way of increasing sales?

    A Marketing should emphasise the high standard of goods.
    B Efforts should be made to increase the number of products.
    C Pricing should be used as an incentive to existing customers.

27 Concerning staffing levels, the group agrees to recommend that

    A certain staff should be redeployed.
    B staff who leave should be replaced.
    C additional staff should be recruited.

28 What problem concerning shifts is the group going to consider in their next meeting?

    A poor relations between certain workers and supervisors
    B negative reactions to changes in working hours
    C variation in the quality of work on different shifts

29 According to the man, what aspect of communication needs to be improved?

    A   the transmission of information between departments
    B   the ways in which feedback is obtained from customers
    C   the extent to which senior managers consult other staff

30 What decision does the group take regarding communication?

    A   They will propose that the company should appoint a communications officer.
    B   They will make a number of suggestions to the relevant departmental managers.
    C   They will suggest that an existing senior manager is given extra responsibility.

You now have 10 minutes to transfer your answers to your Answer Sheet.

Test 3

SPEAKING   16 minutes

SAMPLE SPEAKING TASKS

PART ONE

In this part, the interlocutor asks questions to each of the candidates in turn. You have to give information about yourself and express personal opinions.

PART TWO

In this part of the test, you are asked to give a short talk on a business topic. You have to choose one of the topics from the three below and then talk for about one minute. You have one minute to prepare your ideas.

> A: **Customer relations:** the importance to a company of reliable customer opinions of products
>
> B: **Staff development:** the importance to a company of developing effective career plans for staff
>
> C: **Business strategy:** how to maintain the confidence of company shareholders

PART THREE

In this part of the test, you are given a discussion topic. You have 30 seconds to look at the task prompt, an example of which is below, and then about three minutes to discuss the topic with your partner. After that, the examiner will ask you more questions related to the topic.

For **two** candidates

> **Reducing Staff Turnover**
>
> You work for the branch of your company that has been identified as having the lowest turnover of staff. You have been asked to suggest ways in which staff turnover could be reduced in the other branches.
>
> Discuss and decide together:
>
> - what the reasons for high staff turnover in a company might be
> - what effect the high staff turnover might have on future methods of selecting staff.

For **three** candidates

Reducing Staff Turnover

You work for the branch of your company that has been identified as having the lowest turnover of staff. You have been asked to suggest ways in which staff turnover could be reduced in the other branches.

Discuss and decide together:

- what the reasons for high staff turnover in a company might be
- what effect the high staff turnover might have on future methods of selecting staff
- what procedures concerning staff induction and training might need to be introduced.

Follow-on questions

- How can employees be affected by a high turnover of staff in their department? (Why?)
- Do you think a high turnover of staff can have a negative effect on customer service? (Why?/Why not?)
- Do you think there are any situations in which high turnover of staff is helpful to a company? (Why?/Why not?)
- Would it be beneficial for companies to bring in new staff to join existing work teams? (Why?/Why not?)
- Do you think people will change jobs more often in the future? (Why?/Why not?)

Test 4

READING   1 hour

PART ONE

Questions 1–8

- Look at the statements below and at the five summaries of articles from a business journal on the opposite page.
- Which summary (**A, B, C, D** or **E**) does each statement (**1–8**) refer to?
- For each statement (**1–8**), mark one letter (**A, B, C, D** or **E**) on your Answer Sheet.
- You will need to use some of these letters more than once.
- There is an example at the beginning (**0**).

Example:

0 This summary offers insights from research into companies with contrasting success rates.

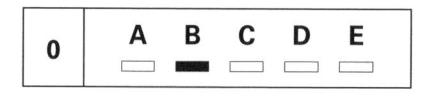

0 A ■ C D E

1 This summary refers to the preference for certain types of customers.

2 This summary refers to the potentially conflicting requirements of customers these days.

3 This summary makes reference to the fact that a certain approach to product development has been adopted globally.

4 This summary highlights the positive impact of placing customers before competitors.

5 This summary focuses on the company's need to regularly assess the financial outlay on both attracting and keeping customers.

6 This summary mentions a concept that explains market forces in general.

7 This summary offers a set of possible models that can be used to tailor product development to suit customer preferences.

8 This summary refers to the use of non-mainstream strategies in certain companies.

A

Companies throughout the world have embraced mass customization in an attempt to provide unique value to their customers in an efficient manner and at a low cost. But many managers have discovered that mass customization can produce unnecessary cost and complexity. In *The Four Faces of Mass Customization*, James H. Gilmore and B. Joseph Pine II provide managers with a framework to help them determine the type of customization they should pursue. Gilmore and Pine have identified four distinct methods to follow when designing or redesigning a product, process or business unit; managers should examine each method for possible insights into how to serve their customers best.

B

Why are some companies able to sustain high growth and others are not? W. Chan Kim and Renée Mauborgne studied high-growth companies and companies in the same field which are doing less well, and found a striking difference in each group's assumptions about strategy. In *Value Innovation: the Strategic Logic of High Growth*, the authors report on companies that have broken with conventional logic to offer customers quantum leaps in value. These companies have focused on what most customers need, instead of on beating their rivals.

C

Increasingly, companies are less focused on selling products and more interested in keeping customers. Ideally, they want to attract and keep only high-value customers. In *Manage Marketing by the Customer Equity Test*, Robert C. Blattberg and John Deighton provide a model to help managers find the optimal balance between spending on acquisition and spending on retention – and thus grow their customer equity to its fullest potential. And because the balance is never static, the authors also offer a series of guidelines to help managers frame the issue.

D

Our understanding of how markets operate is based on the traditional assumption of diminishing returns: products or companies that get ahead in a market eventually run into limitations. But, in recent times, Western economies have undergone a transformation from processing resources to processing information, from the application of raw energy to the application of ideas. As this shift in production has occurred, the mechanisms that determine economic behaviour have also shifted – from diminishing returns to increasing returns. In *Increasing Returns and the New World of Business*, W. Brian Arthur illuminates the differences between the two worlds and offers advice to managers operating in both kinds of markets.

E

Companies currently face a predicament in many mass markets. Customers are demanding that their orders be fulfilled ever more quickly, but they are also demanding highly customized products and services. In *Mass Customization at Hewlett-Packard: The Power of Postponement*, Edward Feitzinger and Hau L. Lee show how HP has proved that a company can deliver customized products quickly and at a low cost by rethinking and integrating the designs of its products, the processes used to make and deliver those products, and the configuration of its supply networks.

PART TWO

Questions 9–14

- Read this advice about responding to questions from the audience while giving presentations.
- Choose the best sentence from the opposite page to fill each of the gaps.
- For each gap (**9–14**), mark one letter (**A–H**) on your Answer Sheet.
- Do not use any letter more than once.
- There is an example at the beginning (**0**).

Taking Questions

When giving presentations, it is common practice to encourage audience involvement and this often takes the form of questions from the floor. A good deal has been written recently discussing the pros and cons of various approaches to handling these. (**0**) .....*H*.....

One approach is to take questions as and when they arise. Usually there are only a few points from the floor but in the event of receiving too many, the presenter may move the presentation on by reminding the audience of the time, and offering to continue the discussion later. (**9**) .... Those who aren't will simply have to wait.

Another approach is to ask for questions after each main point has been addressed. A danger here is that too much time may be sacrificed to questions and, as a consequence, important parts of the message have to be edited out. The audience may also confuse the presenter by asking about points that he or she intends to cover later in the presentation. If this happens, it is important to make the audience aware that any such queries will be dealt with during the course of the session. (**10**) ....

Alternatively, mid-point questions can be discouraged by signalling, during the introduction, that you would prefer questions at the end. If you take this approach, however, it is important to bear in mind that when you get to the end, it may take a little time for people to adjust and to reflect on what they have heard and to formulate a question they want to ask. (**11**) .... To overcome this, it is useful to have a chairperson to direct the proceedings or a colleague 'planted' in the audience who is prepared to ask the first question if necessary. A chairperson can also help by ensuring that questions are taken in turn. This is particularly useful if you have an over-eager questioner who tries to monopolise attention. (**12**) ....

Another potential problem is hostile questioners who ask the kind of question they know will be difficult to answer. This may be done in an attempt to destroy the presenter's case and every effort must be made to limit the damage and to search out opportunities to gain advantage. It is always a good idea to be aware of the traps that this type of questioner may try to set. (**13**) .... Even then, it may be that you do not know the answer, in which case the safest response is to say so. The rest of the audience may appreciate your honesty. It may also be possible to move the attention away from the questioner by asking the rest of the audience if anyone else can provide an answer.

Sometimes members of the audience may attempt to put forward an alternative case or demonstrate their own competence by making a lengthy claim rather than asking questions. (**14**) .... For example: 'Yes, I think we need to bear some of these points in mind. May we have the next question, please?'

Example: 0 — H

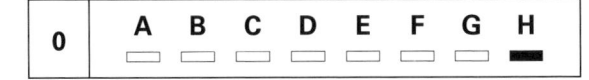

A Other members of the audience may quickly become frustrated if this means that their questions remain unanswered.

B An opportunity may still arise to make the point clearer and eliminate any such ambiguity.

C Acknowledging the statement and then seeking a question from someone else can be an effective way of moving the session on.

D This approach indicates to the audience that answering their questions now might undermine the clarity and structure of the talk.

E A statement such as 'I will come back to this point at the end' should keep most people happy.

F Anticipating potential weaknesses in your argument and how you might respond to questions about them is an important aspect of your preparation.

G There is even the possibility that an embarrassing silence may ensue.

H However, my intention here is simply to present the most common strategies.

PART THREE

Questions 15–20

- Read Stephen Overell's review of a book by Frances Cairncross called *The Insidious Tech Revolution*, and the questions on the opposite page.
- For each question (**15–20**), mark one letter (**A, B, C** or **D**) on your Answer Sheet.

First it revolutionised everything, then it changed nothing and now no one knows what to think. Predictions about how the communications revolution would transform management have followed a trajectory just as wild and erratic as high-technology stock prices. It is timely, then, to read a calm, temperate analysis arguing that we have underestimated the capacity of the internet to transform companies and businesses.

Despite the high expectations of the time, the dotcom business model was never likely to bequeath an enduring legacy of lightning growth and quick cash. Frances Cairncross's contention is that now the frantic energy has been dissipated, the real revolutionary effect of that model on the structures, functions and activities of established businesses and markets can start to become clear. Discerning it can be a subtle affair: 'The most widespread revolution in the workplace will come from the rise in collaboration and the decline of hierarchy,' she writes.

Both of these, of course, were trends-in-progress before the widespread adoption of internet technology. But they are the areas where the change can now be perceived as most profound, precisely because developments in communications technology have worked with the grain of pre-existing movements, accelerating what was already happening. In previous generations, communications flowed from the top of companies downwards. But as more firms began to strip out layers of hierarchy, the internet allowed the flatter corporate architecture and web-like structures of modern organisations to function efficiently. Multifunctional teams, the much-pampered child of 1990s management theory, would be so much trickier to run without the internet. In addition, the internet enables efficient outsourcing and management of external suppliers. Highly marketable workers now have a choice. They can work flexibly if they want to auction their skills to well-paying clients, and move on when they get restless. From a company perspective, the transformed feelings about work among desirable external personnel carry their own difficulties. Many companies are finding that squads of free agents can be difficult to manage and reward. Human resources directors in some sectors are having to behave like theatrical casting agents: they staff work, not jobs.

As Ms Cairncross suggests, new information technology leads to organisational change. Every aspect of running a company, whether building a brand (down to five years from 50), managing an 'ecosystem' of suppliers, innovation, or leading and motivating senior executives, has undergone – and continues to undergo – a transformation. This is not always in predictable ways, though. Who would have guessed that the widespread adoption of email would mean that turning up in person would actually carry greater weight than before?

Predicting the managerial consequences of the communications revolution inevitably risks being a hostage to fortune, especially as the revolution is still in its infancy. The speed of innovation is enough to make most of us feel bewildered. The telephone was invented in the 1870s but it was not until the 1980s that the telephone banking industry took off. Dotcom companies went from boom to bust in just seven years, fragmenting old markets and creating new ones as they went. In such an atmosphere, fortune reading needs to be tempered by prudent vigilance.

15 In the first paragraph, Overell notes that views regarding the impact of the internet on business have

    A adversely affected the stock market.
    B ignored certain important facts.
    C at last been proved wrong.
    D fluctuated over time.

16 What point does Frances Cairncross make about dotcom business?

    A Its real long-term effects were not immediately apparent.
    B It was considered irrelevant by established companies.
    C Its arrival had not been anticipated.
    D It delayed other developments that proved more beneficial.

17 Overell refers to multifunctional teams because they

    A blossomed despite an internet-led corporate culture.
    B triggered the breakdown of organisational hierarchies.
    C exemplify an internal system that operates better with the internet.
    D contradict a widely held theory about the internet.

18 Overell compares human resources directors to casting agents to illustrate his point that

    A companies are struggling to keep their labour costs down.
    B the concept of employment has changed significantly.
    C too many external personnel apply for each available job.
    D the fees demanded for outsourced work are constantly changing.

19 According to the fifth paragraph, what unexpected effect has the internet had?

    A It has raised the profile of poor communicators.
    B It has changed the function of business meetings.
    C It has increased the value placed on face-to-face interaction.
    D It has enabled companies to use a larger number of suppliers.

20 How does Overell end his review?

    A by taking a positive view of the future
    B by recommending caution in predicting the future
    C by showing how luck influences future success
    D by drawing parallels between the past and the future

PART FOUR

Questions 21–30

- Read the article below about promotional discounts.
- Choose the correct word to fill each gap from **A**, **B**, **C** or **D** on the opposite page.
- For each question (**21–30**), mark one letter (**A**, **B**, **C** or **D**) on your Answer Sheet.
- There is an example at the beginning (**0**).

PROMOTIONAL DISCOUNTS FOR CORPORATE CUSTOMERS

Promotional discounts are a form of discount used primarily to (**0**) .... a new product, to try to increase sales of existing products, or to reduce the inventory (**21**) .... of a particular product or products. They can also be employed to (**22**) .... customers to place an extra order, or increase the size of a regular order, so that the order will (**23**) .... for a price reduction. Many companies use this (**24**) .... if their products have seasonal (**25**) .... and troughs. A promotional incentive is a calculated risk that must generate a higher level of orders from customers who don't usually buy in those quantities. If the only result is to encourage buyers to put a large (**26**) .... of discounted products in their warehouse, and reduce the size of the next few orders until they have sold the discounted product, then the promotion has failed to (**27**) .... the desired results.

When problems – particularly problems of communication regarding the (**28**) .... of the discount – occur during the (**29**) .... of a promotion, the person who is managing the credit (whether the owner or a designated employee) will be spending too much extra time responding to the oral and written questions of customers. At this point, the credit manager must put on his or her customer relations hat and move into damage (**30**) .... before it becomes a more serious problem.

82

Example:

| | A | launch | B | declare | C | install | D | proclaim |

0 A ■ B ☐ C ☐ D ☐

21	A	point	B	rank	C	stage	D	level
22	A	instigate	B	motivate	C	provoke	D	initiate
23	A	qualify	B	merit	C	attain	D	rate
24	A	implement	B	application	C	movement	D	tactic
25	A	peaks	B	heights	C	tips	D	caps
26	A	capacity	B	size	C	volume	D	scope
27	A	convey	B	fulfil	C	meet	D	produce
28	A	characteristic	B	nature	C	disposition	D	spirit
29	A	course	B	path	C	route	D	track
30	A	direction	B	manipulation	C	limitation	D	handling

PART FIVE

Questions 31–40

- Read the article below about a British manufacturing company.
- For each question (**31–40**), write one word in CAPITAL LETTERS on your Answer Sheet.
- There is an example at the beginning (**0**).

Example: | 0 | I | N | T | O | | | | |

Manufacturer's new service focus

The huge Eastman chemical complex in Tennessee, USA symbolises the effort by one mid-sized UK manufacturer to make a move (**0**) .... the world of services.

Stationed full-time on the site – which is one of the biggest chemical works in the US – are six employees of British firm AES Seal, (**31**) .... job is to maintain and replace the mechanical seals in rotating machinery throughout the complex. The link with Eastman is part of AES's push to become as much a service company as a manufacturer.

The company has built its service operations by spelling (**32**) .... the direct financial benefits it can offer new customers: (**33**) .... return for a service contract covering a specific site, AES will reduce current maintenance costs by 25%. The company has been able to hit this target up until (**34**) .... and its service contracts account (**35**) .... a respectable proportion of its annual revenue.

However, the added service offering consists (**36**) .... only of the pursuit of individual contracts, but also of trying to build the question of service into AES's overall culture. About a fifth of the company's employees currently work in a service function, advising customers both on the type of seal to buy (**37**) .... on the correct way to operate their plants (**38**) .... that sealing costs are reduced.

Design skills are also central to the operation. AES employs about 25 people to design new seals, vital in helping the operating efficiencies of the companies it sells (**39**) .... Progress is such (**40**) .... AES will soon be scarcely recognisable as the company it used to be.

PART SIX

Questions 41–52

- Read the text below about business schools.
- In most of the lines (**41–52**), there is one extra word. It is either grammatically incorrect or does not fit in with the meaning of the text. Some lines, however, are correct.
- If a line is correct, write **CORRECT** on your Answer Sheet.
- If there is an extra word in the line, write **the extra word** in CAPITAL LETTERS on your Answer Sheet.
- The exercise begins with two examples (**0** and **00**).

Examples:

0	T	H	E	I	R		
00	C	O	R	R	E	C	T

Faculty Sent Out Into Real World

0	As companies downsize by their eliminating managers and combining many
00	functions in one, business schools have also started crossing departmental
41	lines when teaching management. One school where has recently begun
42	selecting and training some of its faculty members so that they can take over
43	some of the school's key accounts from its executive department. Selling the
44	school's executive programmes was used to be the work of a separate marketing
45	division, but from now on it has been decided that the teachers themselves will
46	assume responsibility taken for portfolios from top clients. They will be prepared
47	for their new tasks in a team-teaching seminar and learn how to handle on
48	customer relations. They will also visit companies and see how they do
49	operate. Another important aspect of their training is the reading case studies
50	and learning to negotiate with and design programmes. It is hoped that this
51	project will bring the school closer to the market and boost up revenue. If it
52	proves to be successful, no doubt about other schools will soon begin to adopt
	the same measures.

Test 4

WRITING   1 hour 10 minutes

PART ONE

Question 1

- The bar chart below shows the predicted numbers of participants on three courses at the Wakeley Business College during the coming year. Each course is offered four times a year.
- Using the information from the chart, write a short **report** comparing the predicted enrolments for the three courses for the coming year.
- Write **120–140** words.

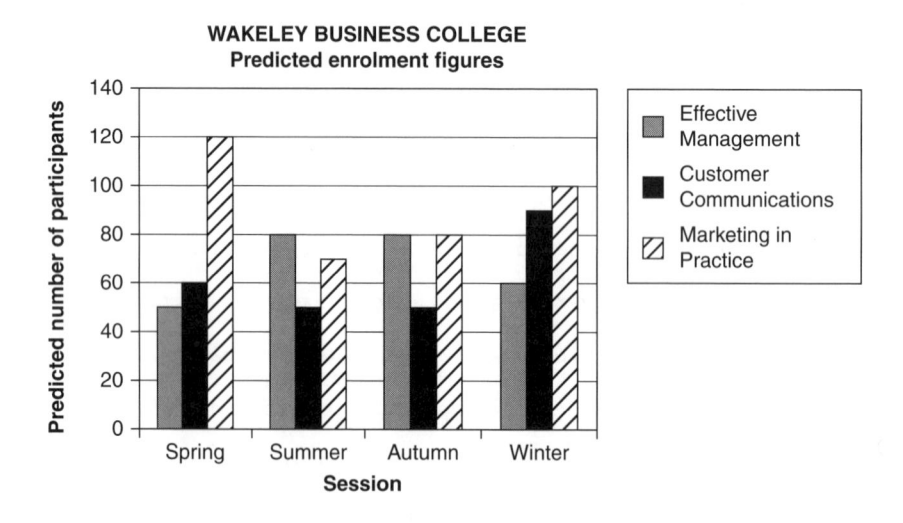

WAKELEY BUSINESS COLLEGE
Predicted enrolment figures

(Bar chart showing predicted number of participants by session)

- Spring: Effective Management 50, Customer Communications 60, Marketing in Practice 120
- Summer: Effective Management 80, Customer Communications 50, Marketing in Practice 70
- Autumn: Effective Management 80, Customer Communications 50, Marketing in Practice 80
- Winter: Effective Management 60, Customer Communications 90, Marketing in Practice 100

PART TWO

Write an answer to **one** of the questions **2–4** in this part. Write your answer in **200–250** words.

Question 2

- One of your company's competitors is about to open a new store close to your most successful retail outlet. Your line manager has asked you to write a report outlining how this will affect your business.
- Write your **report** for your line manager:
    - explaining which types of customers the competitor is targeting
    - describing the possible effects on your company of the competitor's new store
    - suggesting how to deal with the problems arising from this competition.

Question 3

- You work for an established company which would like to expand into new markets. The company has decided to employ a market research organisation to help with this. Your boss has asked you to write to various market research organisations.
- Write a **letter** to be sent to these market research organisations:
    - introducing your company
    - describing what you would like the market research organisation to do
    - explaining how your company intends to use the results of the market research
    - saying how the market research organisation should respond if interested.

Question 4

- The offices of the company where you work are overcrowded. Your head of department has asked you to propose ways of using the office space more effectively.
- Write a **proposal** for your head of department, including the following information:
    - an outline of how the current problem came about
    - some suggestions for how to use the office space more effectively
    - possible difficulties of implementing your suggestions and how these could be overcome.

Test 4

LISTENING Approximately 40 minutes (including 10 minutes' transfer time)

PART ONE

Questions 1–12

- You will hear a college lecturer talking to a group of students about two case studies in Customer Relationship Management (CRM).
- As you listen, for questions **1–12**, complete the notes using up to three words or a number.
- After you have listened once, replay the recording.

Case studies in Customer Relationship Management (CRM)

Unicorn (telecoms company)
- New software means that advisers know the (**1**) .... of a call before answering it.
- The working group investigated the way in which Unicorn's (**2**) .... were used.
- Unicorn's contact centres in different (**3**) .... are connected.
- There was a two-thirds reduction in the number of (**4**) .... across several departments.
- The most significant achievement was an improvement in the (**5**) .... of customers.
- The factors in Unicorn's success include:
  - the involvement of employees
  - a promise of no obligatory (**6**) ....

Northlands Water (water company)
- It was created following the (**7**) .... of several authorities.
- It had to reduce costs, improve service and maintain its (**8**) ....
- It bought its CRM system from Parchment, who also provided its (**9**) .... software.
- The benefits of the new system include:
  - a reduction in the number of (**10**) ....
  - the big, complicated (**11**) .... has been made more efficient
  - the (**12**) .... get information by computer.

PART TWO

Questions 13–22

- You will hear five people talking about the businesses they set up, and about what caused problems in the first year.
- For each extract there are two tasks. For Task One, decide which reason each speaker gives for setting up their own business from the list **A–H**. For Task Two, decide what caused problems in the first year from the list **A–H**.
- After you have listened once, replay the recording.

Task One – Reason for setting up own business

- For questions **13–17**, match the extracts with the reason for setting up a business, listed **A–H**.
- For each extract, choose the reason that the speaker gives.
- Write one letter (**A–H**) next to the number of the extract.

13	Speaker 1	**A**	I had been unsuccessful in previous work.
		B	I was inspired during a temporary posting.
14	Speaker 2	**C**	I followed a family tradition.
		D	I wished to manufacture my own invention.
15	Speaker 3	**E**	I wanted to make good use of what I had studied at college.
16	Speaker 4	**F**	I was approached by a potential backer.
		G	I identified a significant gap in the market.
17	Speaker 5	**H**	I found that suitable premises were available.

Task Two – What caused problems in the first year

- For questions **18–22**, match the extracts with the problems, listed **A–H**.
- For each extract, decide what caused problems in the first year.
- Write one letter (**A–H**) next to the number of the extract.

18	Speaker 1	**A**	labour relations difficulties
		B	inappropriate choice of software
19	Speaker 2	**C**	health and safety issues
		D	inadequate training of workforce
20	Speaker 3	**E**	breakdown of equipment
		F	unexpected competition
21	Speaker 4	**G**	bad recruitment decisions
		H	inefficient data management
22	Speaker 5		

Test 4

PART THREE

Questions 23–30

- You will hear two colleagues, Sam, a production manager, and Julia, his assistant, discussing changes at the furniture manufacturing company they work for.
- For each question (**23–30**), mark one letter (**A**, **B** or **C**) for the correct answer.
- After you have listened once, replay the recording.

23 Sam wants to streamline operations in order to

    A reduce staffing levels in production.
    B be able to sell direct to customers.
    C increase the company's market share.

24 Julia believes that the company's future success will depend on

    A the simplicity of its price structure.
    B the flexibility of its production.
    C the diversity of its product range.

25 Sam wants to use the extra space on the factory floor for

    A work which was previously subcontracted.
    B extra production of core products.
    C housing the company's testing facility.

26 What view does Julia express about the changes the company is making?

    A They will have greater impact in some markets than in others.
    B They should be communicated to customers.
    C They do not go far enough in reducing delivery times.

27 Sam wants to attract market leaders as customers because they

    A will contribute to the company's development.
    B usually negotiate contracts on more favourable terms.
    C will require large orders because of their sales volume.

28 Julia thinks the changes will have a positive impact on staff because

    A they will participate in the company improvements.
    B they will have access to better staff training.
    C they will receive higher salaries due to cost savings.

29 Following the operational changes, Sam intends to

    A reorganise the management structure of the company.
    B invest in improving teamwork and co-operation.
    C recruit skilled design staff to develop new products.

30 According to Julia, what is a key thing to be concerned about?

    A being copied by rival firms
    B achieving goals within time
    C the reaction of markets

You now have 10 minutes to transfer your answers to your Answer Sheet.

SPEAKING   16 minutes

SAMPLE SPEAKING TASKS

PART ONE

In this part, the interlocutor asks questions to each of the candidates in turn. You have to give information about yourself and express personal opinions.

PART TWO

In this part of the test, you are asked to give a short talk on a business topic. You have to choose one of the topics from the three below and then talk for about one minute. You have one minute to prepare your ideas.

> A: **Quality control:** the importance to a company of monitoring the quality of its goods and services
>
> B: **Information management:** how to ensure that information is managed effectively within a company
>
> C: **Financial planning:** the factors involved in deciding on appropriate pricing strategies

PART THREE

In this part of the test, you are given a discussion topic. You have 30 seconds to look at the task prompt, an example of which is below, and then about three minutes to discuss the topic with your partner. After that, the examiner will ask you more questions related to the topic.

For **two** candidates

> ### Staff Recruitment
>
> The retail company you work for is opening new branches nationally and needs to recruit a large number of staff urgently. You have been asked to make recommendations about planning the recruitment.
>
> Discuss and decide together:
>
> - how to attract high-quality staff to the company
> - whether to use an external recruitment agency.

For **three** candidates

Staff Recruitment

The retail company you work for is opening new branches nationally and needs to recruit a large number of staff urgently. You have been asked to make recommendations about planning the recruitment.

Discuss and decide together:

- how to attract high-quality staff to the company
- whether to use an external recruitment agency
- how to ensure that new staff settle into their jobs quickly.

Follow-on questions

- What problems could there be in recruiting a large number of staff at the same time?
- Do you think it's important to recruit staff for a short-term trial period? (Why?/Why not?)
- Do you think new staff should have the same conditions of work as existing staff? (Why?/Why not?)
- How beneficial do you think it is for a company to regularly recruit new staff? (Why?/Why not?)
- Do you think recruitment methods will change in the future? (Why?/Why not?)

KEY

Test 1 Reading

Part 1

1 E   2 D   3 D   4 A   5 C   6 B   7 A   8 E

Part 2

9 C   10 A   11 B   12 D   13 G   14 F

Part 3

15 B   16 A   17 A   18 D   19 C   20 A

Part 4

21 A   22 C   23 D   24 B   25 A   26 D   27 A   28 B   29 D   30 A

Part 5

31 MORE   32 ARE   33 IS   34 NO   35 TO   36 BECAUSE   37 WHEN
38 HAS   39 WHO/THAT   40 IT

Part 6

41 TIME   42 THE   43 HOW   44 REQUIREMENT   45 YET   46 SOME
47 CORRECT   48 JUST   49 TO   50 ON   51 CORRECT   52 US

Test 1 Writing

Question 1

Sample A

> Introduction
> As requested, we are providing you our report about the industrial output from Vietnam during the year 2000 till 2002.
>
> Findings
> State-owned industry has slightly risen from 11% to 13% and stable for the last two years. The none-state industry started close to 20% and has fallen now to 18%. Foreign-invested industry was at 2000 similair as the state-owned industry. However the output has fallen deeply at

the year 2002 but it strengthened in an outstanding turn over at the year 2002. Furthermore with the output from 2002 the losses from 2001 are completely covered.

Conclusion
Generally it can been said that the industrial output from Vietnam is on a good way. In special the state owned and foreign industry.

Recomendation
It is recommended that on deeper examination in the non-state industry is necessary to find out why the output has decreased. Furthermore we should reconsider our investment policy in the foreign invested industry.

Scales	Mark	Commentary
Content	3	All the bar graphs are referred to. However, there are no actual percentages given for foreign-invested industry, but there is indirect reference with *'at 2000 similar to state-owned industry'*. The conclusion and recommendations are irrelevant.
Communicative Achievement	3	The report is written in an appropriate register and format for a report. Straightforward ideas are communicated effectively. The target reader would be informed.
Organisation	3	The text is generally well organised using appropriate headings. A range of linking words are used to good effect (*furthermore, however, but*), but without correct punctuation. There is use of substitution (*it* for *output*).
Language	2	A limited range of grammatical structures are used. Some appropriate vocabulary is used to compare the performances (*slightly risen, stable*). However, this is not always successful (*on a good way, in special*). Errors are present which distract the target reader (*Vietnam is on a good way, in special*).

Sample B

Introduction
The aim of this report is to comment on the annual percentage of industrial output of Vietnam from 2000 to 2002.

Findings
The figures of state-owned industry have slightly incresed from 2000 to 2001 but did not grow any further in 2002.

Whereas none-state industry had reduced its annual increase in 2002 compared to 2001. After having increased by 2% in 2001 figures are now at a slightly lower level than in 2000 an stand now at 19%.

Finally foreign-invested industry has increased hugely in 2002 in comparison

Key

with 2001. The output increased by 7%. After a reduction of 2% in 2001 figures are very promising again in 2002.

Conclusion

State-owned industry is likely to increase slowly but stedily. None-state industry seems to reduce its output in the future, whereas foreign-invested industry is growing rapidly.

Scales	Mark	Commentary
Content	3	All bar graphs are referred to although there are no percentages given for state-owned industry. However, the movement from year to year is correct. The target reader, on the whole, would be informed. The conclusion is irrelevant.
Communicative Achievement	3	The report follows the conventions of format to hold the target reader's attention and gives an early reference to the purpose for writing (*the aim of this report is to comment on*).
Organisation	3	The report is organised using appropriate headings and some simple linking (*but, whereas*), although not always to good effect.
Language	3	A range of vocabulary is used to make comparisons (*compared to, reduction, growing rapidly*). Simple grammatical forms are used with reasonable control (*did not grow any further*). There are some spelling slips (*incresed, stedily*), but these do not impede communication.

Question 2
Sample C

We decided to allow certain of our employees to work at home and so we will follow a model which is already in place in some other countries where our company is located.

The reason behind is that not enough desks are available in our data quality department. I have already spoken to the concerned employees and they will not have a problem to do 90% of their work at home.

It makes sense that everyone of them is coming into the office one day per week, but on different one. For example: employee one on monday and employee two on tuesday, etc. The reason for that is to give feedback to Mr. X (the boss) and to have the possibility to ask open questions.

What is now required from us? We have to make sure that the employees receive laptops and get internet connection at home. When that is given we have only to think about a workplan. One positive aspect is that they don't have to drive the long distance to our office.

All employees of the data quality department are living on the countyside and our office is downtown. Therefore they can save a lot of time which they can use to work accordingly.

The negative aspect is that we can loose control what they are doing at home, duly working for the company? That's why we need to prepare an exact work-plan in advance which we hand out to the employees on the days when the people are in the office.

From my point of view this model will have sucess when we follow the actionplan. However it works we an roll out to another department within the company.

Scales	Mark	Commentary
Content	2	All the content points are addressed. However, the candidate has referred to a future scheme rather than a past one. This would result in some confusion and so, the target reader would not be fully informed.
Communicative Achievement	2	The report uses the conventions of the task to communicate straightforward ideas despite the lack of a clear purpose for writing the report at the beginning.
Organisation	2	The answer is written in appropriate register for a report and the content points are addressed in a logical order, but the text is overparagraphed. Some substitution is used (*they* for employees).
Language	2	Everyday vocabulary is used appropriately. There are some spelling slips (*loose, an roll out*) and errors with prepositions, but these do not generally impede communication. Simple grammatical forms are used with reasonable control (*one positive aspect is that they don't have to drive the long distance to our office*).

Sample D

Report on partial home work of staff members

Introduction

This report aims to clarify the results of our experiment allowing certain employees to work from home for part of the week.

Findings

The reason for this experiment was a demand placed by the staff members themselves. There arguments were that some paper and project work could be done more efficiently at home without been interrupted by collegues and phone calls. Therefore we decided to try this out during an experimental period. For this the following roles were agreed:

* Mondays and Thursdays no home work was allowed. On these days regular meetings would be hold
* At least six staff members have to be in the office during the day.
* Each staff member could be reached by phone. This in case of an emergency.

During the time of the experiment it was found that the biggest profit was the time savings and therefore the increase in productivity. Employees felt also less stressed and more motivated.

We experienced some problems with defining on which days who would be working at home and also the planning of the meetings worked not so well.

Key

> Conclusion and Recommendations
>
> As conlusion we highly recommend this scheme. The above mentioned problems have already been solved. Thanks to the increase in motivation and productivity the company will also see direct benefits in teh near future.
>
> We are shure that this new working scheme will also attract new applicants and influence positively our image as employer.

Scales	Mark	Commentary
Content	3	Most of the content is relevant and the points tend to be expanded. However, the fourth content point (making a recommendation) is not expanded on effectively and so the target reader would not be fully informed.
Communicative Achievement	3	The conventions for the communicative task are generally used appropriately (*this report aims to clarify the results of our experiment*) and it holds the target reader's attention.
Organisation	3	The text is generally well-organised and uses appropriate headings (*introduction, findings, conclusion and recommendations*). It also makes use of a limited number of bullet points which are appropriate to this task.
Language	3	A range of vocabulary is used appropriately (*efficiently, profit, productivity and motivated*). It uses a range of simple structures with control (*at least six staff members have to be in the office during the day*). A number of errors are present (*shure, without been interrupted*), but these do not impede communication.

Question 3

Sample E

> Dear Sirs,
>
> I am writing with reference to Order 50/52/01 which I received from you yesterday. Unfortunately, I must complain about the quality of the goods and delay in delivery.
>
> My company has been purchasing the stationery you offer for few years now. So far, we have not encountered any serious problems. But this time I have no choice, but to inform you about the situation.
>
> The pencils you delivered were broken and pens were of different kind than we ordered. Moreover, the boxes were marked incorrectly. The consignment arrived two days after agreed date, which caused us inconvenience, because we had promised our customers early delivery.
>
> Last month we ignored the fact that the exercise books you had delivered were of different colours that expected. But this time we are going to send you all the goods back. They should be replaced and delivered to us as soon as possible. What is more, we must ask you for a 15% discount.

Unless the problem is solved quickly, we will have to undertake legal steps, as this kind of situation is unacceptable.

Please treat the matter as urgent.

We are looking forward to your prompt reply.

Yours faithfully,

Purchasing Director.

Scales	Mark	Commentary
Content	3	All points are covered and are relevant to the task. The target reader would be informed. However, the final content point (stating what will happen if the situation does not improve) could have been expanded.
Communicative Achievement	4	Uses the conventions of the task to hold the reader's attention and communicate straightforward ideas (*the pencils you delivered were broken and pens were of different kind than we ordered*). It is formal and polite without being threatening.
Organisation	4	The text is written in an appropriate register and format for a letter with an early reference to the reason for writing and a suitable closing (*we are looking forward to your prompt reply*). Cohesive devices are used well.
Language	3	Uses a range of lexis and structures (*last month we ignored the fact that the exercise books you had delivered were of different colours*). However, there are a few non-impeding errors (*for few years, were of different kind*).

Sample F

Dear Mr. or Mrs,

since 10 years your company delivers us goods for our workplace. We get all papers, pens, letter-paper, rubbers and other things you need in the office day to day from you. I can not remember that we had any kinds of problems with you reguarding the delivery. But now, since more or less 5 times we are very angry about you, because when we had ordered the things we were needing, we get wrong things or we get not so much we have ordered. One time the paper were blue and not red, like we have ordered.

You have to know that we could not do our work very well, if things like these happen. We want to make you a solution, how we can handle these problems.

So if we send you an order with the products we are needing, you have to send back a massage with the products we are needing. But do not send back our order, please send a new massage back, where you have filled in our product order. Because than we know, that you have read our order completly.

If the situation does not improve we have to cut our contract and we have to look for a new supplier. I hope that this situations is not coming, because the years ago our behaviour was very well. So please be so kind and change the situation

Best regards

Key

Scales	Mark	Commentary
Content	3	All the content points are addressed and the target reader would be on the whole informed.
Communicative Achievement	1	The text communicates simple ideas in a generally appropriate way. The register is not entirely appropriate (*we are very angry about you*).
Organisation	2	The letter is organised using paragraphs with the content points expressed in a logical order. Some basic linking words are used (*because, and*) although *because* is overused. The opening and closing are not wholly appropriate (*Dear Mr or Mrs, Best regards*).
Language	0	Both grammatical structure and spelling errors are distracting and some are impeding (*send a new massage back, I hope that this situations is not coming*).

Question 4

Sample G

To: Training Director
From:
Date: 26.11.2005
Subject: Business training

Reasons

We have 3 different courses which we could offer our employees. Appraising staff, software Applications and Effective Presentations.

Recommendations

First of all, every course causes the equal amount of costs. In that reason, I compare which course would be the most effective. Secondly, we need a large number of staff who want to take part in the recommended course. I suggest, we offer the software Applications course, because this is the fast increasing area in our business and everybody should be interested in the new technology. In the daily business I realise how fast the technology is changing.

In addition to that course, our board of directors may visit the course for presentations skills. They would have benefits because they are often in public and have to know how to communicate to the clients. Furthermore, the course for Appraising Staff will not be offered. Our surveys have shown that the relationship between employees has been perfect.

Possible drawbacks

It may have a number of staff who prefers to work instead of visite a course. In that reason, I would offer the courses by e-mail and the members may register or not, what means that the candidates who are coming, are motivated to reach their personaly goals.

Scales	Mark	Commentary
Content	2	The target reader is only partly informed due to minor omissions. Point 1 is partially addressed as a course is identified, but it is not clear that this is the course the writer would like to attend (*and everybody should be interested in the new technology*). Also, the final content point, although addressed, is confusing as 'appraising' (in the rubric) appears to have been misunderstood.
Communicative Achievement	3	It uses the conventions of a proposal to communicate straightforward ideas and holds the target reader's attention.
Organisation	3	The text is organised in paragraphs and is connected and cohesive in parts using some linking devices (*first of all, in addition, furthermore*). There are headings, but these are not always appropriate (*reasons*).
Language	2	There is an adequate range of grammatical forms used, but errors are quite frequent. The errors are mainly non-impeding (*it may have a number of staff*), but some are slightly confusing (*every course equals the amount of costs*).

Sample H

INTRODUCTION
I am submitting this proposal in order to analaze the different courses that the company is considering to provide to our employees. First of all, I belive that this decision is going to benefit the company specially in two important aspects: staff motivation and staff qualifications.

APPRASING STAFF
As a Human resources manager, I would like to attend the Apprausing staff course. Interpersonal relationships are very complicated and I would like to take this course because I suppost that it would be useful for my department.

GIVING EFFECTIVE PRESENTATION
Mark Smith, our Sales Manager, is organizing a spead event to present our new product. At the begining he thought about hiring a marketing

Key

agancy to help him with the organization. However marketing agencies are very expensive. I strongly belive that the course about giving effective presentations would help him and his staff. to organize a more attractive .conferance to our clients.

SOFTWARE APPLICATIONS

In the last two years our company has invested a lot of money in new technonlogy. As a result of this fact, last year we created a new information Department. Morover, the company hired new technicians what represented a substancial inversion.

According to the current situation of the company, I think that it should not continue investing in the same area this is the main reason why I belive that a course about software applications would not be useful.

CONCLUSION

As a conclusion, I think that the company should choose the Appraising staff course and the course about giving effective presentations. Both courses are going to be profitable in many different ways.

Scales	Mark	Commentary
Content	5	All the content is relevant and expanded appropriately. The target reader would be fully informed.
Communicative Achievement	4	The proposal is written in an appropriately formal register following the conventions of format and it has a positive effect on the target reader.
Organisation	4	The text is well-organised using appropriate headings including an introduction and conclusion. However, the conclusion is not a content point and so is unnecessary. It uses a number of linking devices (*first of all, as a result, at the beginning, however*). It also uses substitution effectively (*he and him* for *Mark Smith*).
Language	3	Some simple and complex grammatical forms are used with control (*is organizing a spread event to present our new product*). There is some good use of relevant vocabulary (*interpersonal relationships*). Some spelling and punctuation slips are present (*Apprasing, suppost, belive, agancy,*) but these do not impede communication.

Test 1 Listening

Part 1

1. 24
2. PLANNING
3. LEAD (THE GROUP)
4. (PERSONAL) QUALITIES
5. PRESENTATION(S)
6. STEALING
7. (NAME) BADGES
8. (GROUP) ACTIVITIES
9. RECEPTION
10. BRANCH
11. MANAGEMENT TRAINING PROGRAMME
12. INFORMATION PACK(S)

Part 2

13 D 14 E 15 B 16 G 17 C 18 F 19 A 20 D 21 B 22 E

Part 3

23 C 24 B 25 B 26 A 27 A 28 C 29 C 30 B

Tapescript

Listening Test 1

This is the Business English Certificate Higher 5, Listening Test 1.

Part One. Questions 1 to 12.

You will hear the head of recruitment at Buyright Supermarkets plc talking to a group of job applicants who are attending the company's assessment centre. Here they will be assessed for places on Buyright's training programme.

As you listen, for questions 1 to 12, complete the notes, using up to three words or a number.

After you have listened once, replay the recording.

You now have 45 seconds to read through the notes.

[pause]

Now listen, and complete the notes.

[pause]

Good morning, and welcome to the Buyright Supermarkets assessment centre. My name is Jackie Shellens, and I'm the head of recruitment. I'll be looking after you for these two days.
 As you know, we've invited you here to choose ten of you for places on our management training programme. Of the original seventy applicants, we've shortlisted you twenty-four to go through this assessment process, which I'll outline now.
 You'll be taking part in six main activities this evening and tomorrow: a team discussion, team challenge, psychometric tests, individual interview, presentation and simulations. You'll be given more detailed information about each before you do it, but I'll just outline them briefly.

Key

First, the two team activities: for the discussion you'll be given a problem involving planning, and you'll have to find a solution in a group of six. In the same group, you will have team challenges and you'll take turns to lead the group. These will take place outside, and will include crossing a snake pit without getting bitten – don't worry, they aren't real snakes! – and rounding up a flock of sheep, where you'll be playing the roles of the sheep, sheepdogs and shepherd.

The psychometric tests are written tests and they will take you a couple of hours. You'll be interviewed individually by two people, and they'll focus on your personal qualities, using the psychometric tests as a starting point. The same two people, and the rest of your group of six, will be the audience for the presentations we've asked you to prepare.

For the simulations, you'll be in threes. You'll be given a typical situation in a supermarket – like dealing with a worker suspected of stealing. Two of you will act this out while the third observes, and then you'll discuss what happened and what should be done. Don't worry, it isn't as difficult as it sounds, and we certainly don't expect you to be perfect managers yet!

You've probably noticed that you've been given red, yellow, blue or green name badges, and they're the four groups we've put you into. When I've finished talking to you, the four groups will go off to different rooms, where you'll be given the timetable of group activities and do some icebreaking exercises to get to know each other. At six thirty, there'll be a reception in the West Room, followed by dinner. After that, we'll be having a question-and-answer session with a panel of branch managers, so you'll be able to find out what it's like working for Buyright. Tomorrow will start with breakfast at eight, and the activities will go on until five thirty.

We hope to make our final selection of ten people for the management training programme very soon, and we'll write to you all within a week.

Oh, if you haven't claimed your travel expenses yet, don't forget to fill in your expenses claim form – there should be one in your information pack – and give it to me before you leave.

Now we'll get each group off to the right room, and make a start . . .

[pause]

Now listen to the recording again.

[pause]

That is the end of Part One. You now have 20 seconds to check your answers.

[pause]

Part Two. Questions 13 to 22.

You will hear five different people comparing their last job with their present job.

For each extract, there are two tasks. Look at Task One. For each question, 13–17, choose the reason the speaker gives for leaving their last job, from the list A–H. Now look at Task Two. For each question, 18–22, decide what has surprised them about their new job, from the list A–H.

After you have listened once, replay the recording.

You now have 30 seconds to read the two lists.

[pause]

Now listen, and do the two tasks.

[pause]

Speaker One

| Man: | It wasn't much of a job, so it would be ridiculous to have expected anything like great colleagues or fantastic pay. I'm going to university next year, you see. Anyway, relative to the responsibility the pay was acceptable, but you can stand only so much rudeness from your supervisor, even if you know you're not staying. So I left. Best thing I ever did. Here they offered me better pay and hours and told me I'd be trained, showed me round, which made me feel really welcome. But, what they didn't mention at the beginning, and which is really good, is how much time I'd spend out of the office. I enjoy the regular visits to other branches round the country. I'd stay, if I had to. I really mean that. |

Speaker Two

| Woman: | . . . and then, one day, I thought what I was doing was only tolerable, and I couldn't go on doing it forever because I was never going to get anywhere. It's not that I'm particularly ambitious, but I do want to feel I can progress in a firm, which is why I decided to take this job when it came up. They indicated there were plenty of promotion opportunities. Cantab Electronics is really going places and is famous for having a really creative approach. But when I arrived, I found it was even better than I expected. They said, "Right! Here's what we want to achieve. Come up with your own solutions and submit development plans." Marvellous! It was like being told to do what you liked. |

Speaker Three

| Man: | Well, the salary there was never very good, but that didn't really bother me. What got to me was that I was expected to put in far too much extra time and I was exhausted. So I asked a former colleague, 'If you could choose any company, who would you work for?' He said, 'Startright Recruitment. They're good to work for, and I like the people there. If you're looking for a bit more responsibility, try them.' So I did. You can imagine how I felt when I looked at my December pay slip and discovered I'd been paid an extra thirty per cent though I'd only been with them for a couple of months. The boss said to all of us, 'We've had a good year. Let's all share it!' |

Speaker Four

| Woman: | Actually I could see the way things were going. Orders were down and the company wasn't responding to market changes. So I got out. And I wasn't the only one, though I was one of the first. In fact, about thirty people left. Anyway, I got the interview with this company within a week and I got a good feeling as I walked in the door – everything clean and everyone obviously working very hard. Although it was a new field for me, I'm now reskilled. What's more, I couldn't believe how generous the annual leave is; it's so much time off compared to before. |

Speaker Five

| Man: | Vistatours were surprised I left, I think. After twenty years as Operations Director, people thought I was going to stay forever. But I had to look to the future. I was finding the job too much: everything landed on my desk; I had to take all the decisions. So I resigned one particularly awful day, and didn't even get a leaving present. The very evening I left, the phone rang. It was Orbitravel offering me this job, with a clear job description – which is more than I'd had hitherto – and a comparable salary. I accepted it. I was really afraid when I turned up on the first day that as an outsider I might be resented, but no. Everyone made me feel really at home, and it's working out very well. |

[pause]

Now listen to the recording again.

Key

[pause]

That is the end of Part Two.

Part Three. Questions 23 to 30.

You will hear Mark Finch, a well-known business consultant, speaking to a group of business people at a seminar.

For each question, 23–30, mark one letter (A, B or C) for the correct answer.

After you have listened once, replay the recording.

You now have 45 seconds to read through the questions.

[pause]

Now listen, and mark A, B or C.

[pause]

Woman:	I'm very glad to introduce Mark Finch. I'm sure you've all been looking forward to meeting such a well-respected consultant. Before we take some other questions, could I begin by asking you what general advice you would give to people planning to start a new business?
Mark:	Business is about three things. The first thing is people. You need to make sure that you're going to work with people who've got the right attitude. Commitment outweighs paper qualifications. The second thing is money. You can read a lot of books about exactly how much capital you need to get you through the first couple of years, and so on, but how much that matters depends on which particular kind of business you're going into. The third thing is time. Nothing is more vital than taking time to plan properly. Check out your idea with friends and contacts, look at your local competitors, study costs and prices. That's the most useful thing you can do.
Woman:	I see. Now, a lot of people worry about the dangers of business.
Mark:	Business is not a safe world; it's full of risks. It's always going to be a gamble. You must be prepared to work long hours and to keep doing that until the business becomes successful, however long that might happen to take. Even then you can't relax as, especially if you're providing a service, you have to deal with the often very quick fluctuations in the market.
Woman:	Thank you. Now let's take a question from the audience. Jane?
Jane:	In my company, we're having problems dealing with complaints. Would you recommend a computerised system?
Mark:	A few years ago, I worked with an energy company on this problem. They had computerised their complaints processing because they were receiving so many complaints. But the staff who had to input the data hadn't had enough help with using computers, so the process wasn't working well at all.
Jane:	So what would you recommend to managers?
Mark:	I would say to managers from that example that a computer system in itself will not deal with your problems. Don't just tell your staff to do things, listen to what they have to say about what they need.

Woman:	And the next question, Bill?
Bill:	My company's worried about our high staff turnover. Can you give me some advice?
Mark:	I've recently been working with a car repair company who go out to people's cars, rather than customers bringing their cars to them. But they were having problems with their mechanics. The managers were sending out a newsletter every month full of future plans and aims, but very few of the workers were actually reading it. When I talked to the workers, I found what they really needed was to be appreciated for what they did, to feel that management took an interest. So, I helped the company to bring management and workers closer together, to understand each other better.
Bill:	And that helped to reduce the turnover of staff?
Mark:	Yes, happier staff meant they stopped leaving. This reduction had various benefits, especially improving customer satisfaction so that less publicity was required. With a more constant staff of mechanics, the need for training was significantly reduced.
Woman:	One more question. Pamela?
Pamela	We've recently launched a new product, but it's not selling well, and this is causing a lot of stress throughout the company. Is this a common problem?
Mark:	Well, ok, I'm working with a kitchen equipment manufacturer at the moment. Obviously, I can't give too much detail, but they came up with a new kind of toaster last year. They developed it themselves, and it certainly is a good product, which could really help that company's profitability. They asked me if I thought the problem was delivery costs and times, but I told them to bring in a proper sales manager to upgrade their ability in actually selling the toaster.
Woman:	So we're not alone in this?
Mark:	Oh no, stress is a common problem, and the solution depends on your situation. There are many causes of stress in business. Personally, rather than trying to prevent it, I think you should embrace it. Successfully managed stress can actually make you work more effectively.
Woman:	Mark, thank you very much.

[pause]

Now listen to the recording again.

[pause]

That is the end of Part Three. You now have ten minutes to transfer your answers to your Answer Sheet.

[pause]

Note: Teacher, stop the recording here and time ten minutes. Remind students when there is **one** minute remaining.

[pause]

That is the end of the test.

Key

Test 2 Reading

Part 1

1 A 2 E 3 D 4 B 5 C 6 A 7 B 8 A

Part 2

9 A 10 G 11 C 12 E 13 F 14 B

Part 3

15 A 16 D 17 B 18 C 19 C 20 A

Part 4

21 C 22 B 23 D 24 A 25 B 26 D 27 C 28 A 29 B 30 D

Part 5

31 DESPITE 32 WHICH 33 FOR 34 THOUGH / IF 35 NO
36 WHAT 37 ON 38 THAT 39 NOT 40 IN

Part 6

41 WAY 42 AND 43 ON 44 SOME 45 CORRECT 46 THERE
47 SO 48 SHOULD 49 EXACT 50 CORRECT 51 AS 52 UP

Test 2 Writing

Question 1

Sample A

> Introduction
> The aim of this report is to compare the number of the permanent full-time, the part time and the temporary contract employees of Radnor Design from 2004 to 2007.
>
> Background
> The graph shows the changes of the number of these three types of employees over a four-year period.
>
> Findings
> First of all, permanent part-time employees of Radnor Design have gradually decreased from 380 to 250 in this period. On the other hand, the permanent full-time employees have been increased. They were 200 at the begining of 2004, and slowly inceased its number

until the end of 2006, then rapidly increased in 2007 to over 400. As for the temporary contract employees, their number doesn't seem to be stable. The number increased from 120 to 220 then dropped to 130 over a 2 year – year period in 2004 to 2005. Later on, the number moved simillerly in 2006–2007.

Conclusion
The company seems to have more permanent full-time employees than permanent part-time ones. Also, they use temporary contract employees depending on the situation.

Scales	Mark	Commentary
Content	3	The target reader is, on the whole, informed. However, the final rise for Temporary Contract Employees is not evident in the answer.
Communicative Achievement	4	The report uses the convention of the task to communicate ideas effectively. An early reference to the purpose of writing helps to inform the target reader (*the aim of this report is to compare the number of*).
Organisation	3	Appropriate headings are used to good effect. The text is connected and coherent using some simple linking words (*first of all, on the other hand*).
Language	3	Simple grammatical forms (mainly past simple and present perfect) are used with good control. Some spelling slips are evident (*incleased, simillerly,*) but these do not impede communication.

Sample B

The line graph shows the number of permanent full-time, permanent part time and temporary contract employees. The period under review is from 2004 to 2007.

Permanent part-time employees have a sharp fall of about 60 in 2004, than the number of permanent part-time employees decrease in 2005 up to 350 and since 2006 there is a significant fall down to 250 until 2007.

Permanent full-time employees started with a number of about 200 in the year 2004 and the number decrease significantly up to 280 in 2006.
In year 2007, there is a sharp decrease up to more than 400 permant full-time employees which is the highest number of employees compared with the other one.

In addition, the temporary contract employees shows an up-and-down curve from 2004 to 2007.

Key

Scales	Mark	Commentary
Content	2	Point 3 is not adequately addressed (*shows an up-and-down curve*) and the target reader would not be fully informed.
Communicative Achievement	2	The report communicates simple ideas in a generally appropriate way.
Organisation	1	The text is connected using simple linking words (*and, in addition*) and short paragraphs.
Language	2	The report uses simple grammatical forms with a degree of control. A number of confusing errors are present in the paragraph about Permanent Full Time Employees (*there is a sharp decrease up to*). There is also evidence of basic errors in description of movement (*an up-and -down curve*).

Question 2

Sample C

Report: The outcomes of the visit to Outlet 1

Introduction:

The aim of this report is to show the outcomes of the visit made by staff members from the head office to Outlet 1 last week, analyse its performance and suggest improvements to this retail outlet.

Feedback

The store was with only a few costumers at the moment of the visit but staff members informed us that is common to get busy. It was noticed that some light bulbs were flashing and the staff room door broken.

The clothes were well organized and the staff seemed very happy and friendly. However, despite being aware of the visit, none of them were wearing the uniform provided by the company.

It was also noticed the lack of knowledge by the sales staff about the range of products specially about the new shoes line.

Suggestions

It is strongly suggested the repair of the structural problems noticed, such as the light bulbs and the door. And it is also of enourmous importance that the staff receive training on how to describe and sell products; and is also important that a special training is given in order to cover their lack of knowledge in the range of products.

Scales	Mark	Commentary
Content	3	All the content points are addressed and given equal importance. The target reader would be on the whole informed.
Communicative Achievement	3	Straightforward ideas are communicated well using an appropriate format and register. The report holds the target reader's attention.
Organisation	3	The report is generally well-organised and coherent with an effective use of headings and some basic linking words *(however, also)*.
Language	3	A range of grammatical forms are used with some degree of control. There are a number of errors present *(The store was with only a few costumers, it is strongly suggested the repair of)*. However, there is also evidence of complex grammar being used correctly *(However, despite being aware of the visit, none of them were wearing the uniform provided by the company)*.

Sample D

Performance evaluation – High fashion retail store – Oxford Street

The visit took place on Saturday 10.5.2007, 2.30 pm.

The outlet covers an area of approximately 150 square meters. The main products sold are high-fashion brand label garments and clothes aimed at male and female middle-class and high-income customers.

At the time there were three members of customer service staff present as well as the branch manager. Two of the employees were operating cashiers.

The general attitude of the team was friendly, helpful and professional, however they were not able to handle all customers with the dedication and individually as we expect given our policies for high-fashion outlets.

Furthermore there were a great number of European customers entering the store, mainly French and German.

The main suggestions for improvement from the observations made are:

After discussions with the branch manager I have come to the conclusion that a further two members of customer service staff should be recruited. The new members of staff should preferably speak French and German as second or first language to meet the needs of the majority of our European customers.

All staff should take part in a half-day training session to improve there ability on customer care.

Moreover, there is a drastic need for redecoration and modernisation to keep in touch with changing trends and attitudes of our highly fashion sensitive customers.

I would expect that these improvements are implemented not later than June. 08

Key

Scales	Mark	Commentary
Content	5	All content is relevant and two of the points are expanded with some detail so that the target reader is fully informed.
Communicative Achievement	5	The report uses the convention of the communicative task to hold the target reader's attention and communicate both straightforward and complex ideas effectively (*I would expect that these improvements are implemented not later than June. 08*)
Organisation	4	The text is well organised in a series of paragraphs which logically address the content points and there is a title and a conclusion. The text is connected and coherent using substitution (*they* for *staff*) and linking words (*however, moreover, furthermore*).
Language	4	There is a range of everyday and subject specific vocabulary (*customer service staff, cashiers*) used appropriately including evidence of collocation and a range of adjectives (*drastic need, aimed at, dedication, redecoration, modernisation*). The errors are largely due to ambition and do not impede communication.

Question 3
Sample E

Dear Ladys and Gentlemen

I am writting you to inform you that our company is looking for a new distribution company.

We are a well-known food company, which produces convinience food and which sells our products to retailers e.g. to "Spar" or "Biller".

We have to handle very carefully with our products, so the transport to distribute our products has to be very carefully too. Whereas other companys want to decrease their sale figures, we are very Interested in high quality and in this case, the transport has to be fast, the products, which are frozen, have to arrive frozen by our retailers too, so it must be added that the transport vehicles need a freezer too.

Our company is looking for a changement in transport requirements in the next few years i.t. an extraordinary puncuallity too.

If it is possible I would like to receive detailed information about your distribution company. for example which high standart of transport you want to achieve, in which part of the country you are not able to deliver and if it is possible to transport our products to our retailers on sunday afternoon too?

For every additional service, your company can offer to us, our company would be able to pay a speciall fee too.

I hope, that you are interested in our company, so that we can arrange a meeting.

Sincerely

Scales	Mark	Commentary
Content	2	Content point 3 is not adequately addressed and the target reader would not be informed of how the transport requirements are likely to change in the next few years (*changement*). Point 1 is minimally addressed.
Communicative Achievement	2	The conventions of the communicative task are generally used appropriately. However, the opening (*Dear Ladys and Gentlemen*) is inappropriate.
Organisation	2	The text is organised using paragraphs but some of these are single sentences. The content points are covered in a logical order.
Language	2	A limited range of simple grammatical forms are used with some control. Errors are noticeable but the meaning can still generally be determined (*we have to handle very carefully with our products, convinience food, high standart*).

Sample F

Dear Sirs,

I am the Personnal Assistant to the Managing Director of PHL, the leading pharmaceutical company in the south of Switzerland. PHL was established in 1968 and is specialized in the production of a wide range of multivitamines. Our products are sold in more than 40 countries, where we work with exclusive representatives.

Throughout Europe, the distribution of our products from our plant is done by trucks. It is our endeavour to guarantee our sole agents abroad delivery of the goods within one week, which obviously sometimes is quite a daunting logistical challenge.

Due to recent problems with our present transport company, we are looking for a new reliable partner to work with. Since we intend to expand our export activities to Eastern Europe countries as well, we seek a company that is able to gradually increase capacity during the next few years. Furthermore, one of our utmost criteria is flexibility apart from reliability. Please let us know if, in principle, you are interested in such a long-term cooperation.

At the same time, we kindly request you to send us your latest annual report, details about your car park, capacities as well as some references of companies you have been working with for several years. Please let us also have your price list.

If you need any further information, please do not hesitate to contact me. You can reach me under phone no....

Looking forward to hearing from you soon, I remain,

Yours sincerely

Key

Scales	Mark	Commentary
Content	4	All the content is relevant and most is expanded, but the second content point (describing the transport requirements) is a little vague. On the whole, though, the target reader would be informed.
Communicative Achievement	5	The format and, particularly, the register are wholly appropriate to the task. The response communicates straightforward and complex ideas effectively *(which obviously sometimes is quite a daunting logistical challenge, please let us know if, in principle, you are interested)*. This range of language holds the target reader's attention throughout.
Organisation	4	The text is a well-organised letter using paragraphs with a range of linking devices including substitution (*where* for *countries*) (*furthermore, due to, at the same time, since*).
Language	4	The letter uses a range of appropriate lexis and a relatively wide range of grammatical structures (*daunting logistical challenge, reliable partner to work with*), with a good degree of accuracy. The errors are mainly due to ambition and do not impede communication.

Question 4

Sample G

Proposal for relocating

Purpose:

The aim of this proposal is to outline the reasons for relocating our offices to different premises outside the city.

It also describes the premises we would require and shows the impacts of the relocation on our staff and on the company's business.

Reasons for relocating:

The main reason that has to be pointed out, is the fact that the rent for office spaces in the city centre has been rising constantly over the last five years and just won't go in line with our budget plans for the future. What's more, as we consider to recruit more staff, there is not enough office space available in the city centre.

Description of premises that will be required:

Our new office spaces should be reachable comfortably by public transportation.

The main target, I suggest is that we bring all employees from the three small offices in the city together on one floor. So we'll have to look for ideally a whole building, where it is also possible for us to have enough office space for our new hired employees in future.

What is also required is a canteen, as our staff will not have the possibility to go for lunch in the city because of the longer distance.

Possible impact on staff:

For some of our employees it might be a problem as I know that they live in the city with their family and really enjoyed their short way to the office.

But a positive aspect would be that if all employees work in the same building it will strengthen their team spirit and gives them the opportunity to know each other better, which was not possible before.

Possible impact on the company's business

In the light of the mentioned financial reasons, we would save a lot of money which we could spend more on the educational side. That will motivate and educate our employees and increase the profitability of our company.

Plan of action:

I suggest that we agree on relocating our business, proceed in finding appropriate locations and take further steps such as informing our clients and staff.

Scales	Mark	Commentary
Content	4	All content is relevant and the points are expanded equally so that the target reader is fully informed.
Communicative Achievement	4	The formal register and persuasive tone are appropriate for a proposal and hold the target reader's attention effectively (*in light of the mentioned financial reasons, we would save a lot of money*).
Organisation	4	The text is well organised with an early purpose stated for writing (*the aim of this proposal is*). It uses appropriate headings for each content point. There is also evidence of substitution (*that* for *money saved*) and simple cohesive devices (*but, so, what's more*).
Language	4	The proposal uses a range of simple and complex grammatical forms with a good degree of control (*But a positive aspect would be that if all employees, the rent has been rising constantly*). Errors are infrequent and non-impeding.

Sample H

PROPOSAL:-

This proposal is on the Relocate the office to different premises outside of the city.

Our company having these small offices in the city centre. So I think our company needs to relocate. because. small office. we are facing so many problems. Not only staff members. The customers also. it's a big city and our shop is in centre. The High class coustomers are comming tour office by car. for parking we need place. if they park in front of company, the main road blocked. already Trafic police has given complaint on us. For parking reason some of the coustomers are not intresed to come our Company. So. if we think Relocate again in city centre with big office. So its need more place. Normally in city's cost of place is more. Compare to outside of the city. So my proposal is Relocate the office in out side of the City.

If we Relocate out side. we can give big advirtisements in center of city. Then we can easily improve our company name and staff members are feel to comfortable.

In Citys Traffic 3 am is very high. so due to this reason we are planning 2 hour before to come here. if suppose office time is at 9 then we are starting 7 am clock itself after duty complted. or if we finished our work at 5 clock. we are reaching at 7 pm or sometimes 9 pm. So this also one Reason. So if Relocate our company out side of the city this problem will solve.

Our company having small offices. In this office. we having files, to keep in good manner it. time taking process . if we want to move 2 or 3 persons its mean go to out side from our chamber. its not comfortable. So we are feeling that we are in a Jail. We don't have 1 common Room. because. for lunch where we are working there it self we are taking. So. we need a common Room. for Rest. or whe we have break. For all these things we are requesting to &amp my proposal is Relocate the office in our side of the city.

It seems to be a small problems but. These things only become. main reason for us.

There is a possible move on staff. If they stay city out side. They will feel comfort because out side of city environment is good. in citys. high.

> Air. water. pollution. Some problems also in there but we need keep our health in good condition. And staff familes members also no problem to stay out side of the city. if we have any work we will go Saturday and Sundays. &amp in week ends.
>
> If we Relocate the office in out side of city, there is no problem for company business. because. there is no problems for staff members and coustomers also. so. we have to improve &amp grow our company business.

Scales	Mark	Commentary
Content	1	The target reader is only minimally informed due to content omissions. Point 3 is not entirely successful as it assesses the impact of the move on staff to their health and the environment. Point 4 is also only partially addressed as it assesses the move on the company's business as having (*no problem*). Also, the type of premises required (content point 2) is implied rather than explicit.
Communicative Achievement	1	The proposal uses the convention of the task to communicate straightforward ideas in a generally appropriate way.
Organisation	1	The text is organised through the use of paragraphs although there are errors with punctuation, especially the overuse of full stops, and capitalisation. There is some use of simple cohesive devices (*so*).
Language	0	There are numerous errors which impede meaning (*The High class coustomers are coming tour office by car, for parking we need place.*) The target reader would not understand the proposal.

Test 2   Listening

Part 1

1 BRAND
2 (THE) CORPORATE
3 (OF) NETWORKS (ARE) / NETWORK (IS)
4 SERVICES FOR CUSTOMERS / CUSTOMER CARE SERVICE(S) / CUSTOMER CARE / CUSTOMER SERVICE(S) / SERVICES FOR CLIENTS
5 TECHNICAL EXPERTISE
6 HONEST / FRIENDLY
7 ADVERTISING / ADVERTIZING
8 DELIVERY TIME(S)
9 DATA TRANSMISSION(S)
10 ALLIANCES
11 NEXT GENERATION
12 PENETRATION RATES

Key

Part 2

| 13 C | 14 E | 15 H | 16 A | 17 G | 18 G | 19 B | 20 A | 21 C | 22 D |

Part 3

| 23 B | 24 C | 25 A | 26 A | 27 B | 28 C | 29 C | 30 C |

Tapescript

Listening Test 2

This is the Business English Certificate Higher 5, Listening Test 2.

Part One. Questions 1 to 12.

You will hear a representative of SGC, a telecoms company, giving a talk to a group of business students about SGC.

As you listen, for questions 1 to 12, complete the notes, using up to three words or a number.

After you have listened once, replay the recording.

You now have 45 seconds to read through the notes.

[pause]

Now listen, and complete the notes.

[pause]

I'm very pleased to be able to welcome so many of you. I'll outline SGC's strengths and our strategies for the future and then say a few words about the current state of the market. I'll try to be as brief as I can, and leave time for any questions you may have at the end.

SGC is very well positioned, possessing significant strengths. From our beginning, we've always made promises to have customer-friendly qualities, and this has led to our now having a powerful brand identity wherever we operate. That's something we're committed to maintaining. Within that 'total' approach to all markets in which we have controlled operations, we also have concentrated effectively on the corporate market, and this differentiates us from many of our competitors, who have devoted the majority of their efforts to the limited leisure sector. But it's not all selling – it's what you provide that really matters. That's why we've put so much in the way of time and money resources into setting up networks which operate with great efficiency and precision, and we will always search for ways to eliminate interference and downtime. Our dedicated approach also applies to our recently launched deal in customer care. We've been able to put this together by combining our relationship management resources in order to keep clients assured of the best in service at all times. And last but not least, is innovation, and here our strength is guaranteed by our technical expertise, which is very sophisticated and dynamically managed.

So: a very good current situation. But we won't rest here, and our success will continue to grow as we develop. We want to boost the perceptions of SGC. We feel we are already perceived in the markets as dynamic, as refreshing, and to this we want to add honest and friendly – crucial concepts in the twenty-first century business world. You'll have noticed that we've recently re-packaged our portable products, and we're going to explore previously untried methods of advertising in order to cement this in eye-catching ways. Look out for our message in the most unexpected of places! And one of our selling points is going to be our target to slash broadband call charges, which will come down by over ten per cent in the next half-year, and delivery times, which we aim to bring down by a quarter – thus outdoing all our competitors. As a result, the extra custom and loyalty we believe this will generate will mean a growth in revenues from data transmission, while holding those from commercial transactions steady – no mean feat in a market this competitive. Finally, as we look ahead, we see the path into the future as involving an approach based on co-operation, which is why we'll be setting up a number of alliances. These will be with a variety of appropriate providers and enable truly global penetration.

As for the market, I don't need to tell you that telecoms is a world of often dramatic ups and downturns, but there are some clear opportunities that emerge within the industry. Service providers are competing keenly in terms of the sophistication of the products they package, and so they are migrating from current generation to next generation products in order to be able to offer improvements in capability. This fact alone should guarantee vibrancy in the market. Meanwhile, another exciting opportunity is the rise in revenue sources we should all be seeing as a result of penetration rates, which should soon pass the one hundred per cent mark in some countries.

OK, well, if there are any questions, I'll be happy to answer them . . .

[pause]

Now listen to the recording again.

[pause]

That is the end of Part One. You now have 20 seconds to check your answers.

[pause]

Part Two. Questions 13 to 22.

You will hear five different people talking about workshops they have recently attended.

For each extract, there are two tasks. Look at Task One. For each question, 13 to 17, choose the reason the speaker gives for attending the workshop, from the list A–H. Now look at Task Two. For each question, 18–22, choose the outcome of attending the workshop, from the list A–H.

After you have listened once, replay the recording.

You now have 30 seconds to read the two lists.

[pause]

Now listen, and do the two tasks.

[pause]

Speaker One

Man: There's a danger in business of not seeing the wood for the trees, and I'd been feeling for some time that we were trudging forward with no real sense of why we were doing what we were doing. So before we considered developing new products or services for customers, I wanted to find out more about the reasoning behind development – the ideas and thinking – of systems. That's what this workshop offered. Obviously, I'm not in R and D myself, but I wanted to be able to understand the underlying issues when the R and D people come and talk to me. The workshop made me realise how complex those issues could be, and that's why we've now appointed someone to look after that side of things for the first time.

Speaker Two

Woman: Yes, well I was quite surprised at how big an effect going along to a single afternoon session turned out to have. Afterwards, I spent a few days thinking over what I'd learnt, and talking it through with various colleagues, particularly on the IT team. I concluded we'd been wrong to bring in new sales targets without altering anything else. So we sat down and re-worked people's responsibilities, the definitions of their roles and tasks. Now I think the whole system

Key

works much better. And to think that I only went because I was feeling a bit rusty about the database, and wanted to spend some time trying out how to co-ordinate all the data we'd had on customers. It led me to realise how much more the sales staff could be doing if we re-jigged their role.

Speaker Three

Man: I'm very glad I went to the workshop, as it enabled me to get things moving ahead. If I hadn't gone, I think we'd have ended up calling in outside consultants, which would have been an expensive way to get no more information than we can get by ourselves. But arranging for the HR manager to investigate our staff's expectations and intentions and present it all in writing to the leadership team has worked well enough for our purposes. I signed up for the workshop because I knew we needed to find out more concrete facts about how career patterns are shifting – we can't control them, of course, but if we know about them, we can at least anticipate what's coming. They showed us some case studies, which were really quite similar to our situation.

Speaker Four

Woman: We're in a business where it really is true that you have to keep running even to stand still, and market research keeps showing us that customers expect more and more. The workshop outline said it would cover ways to develop genuinely new products and services, which was exactly what we needed. And it has proved useful. Now that I've put together a dedicated cross-functional group to generate ideas and suggestions, I think we'll start to see some quality results coming through once they're ready to release their findings. And that should give us the competitive edge we so badly need to gain, without the expense of hiring an agency or taking on new staff who we can't accommodate.

Speaker Five

Man: There's certainly been quite a shift over the last few years towards measurement – it seems everything has to be quantified these days. We've been measuring an ever-widening scope of aspects of the business, and so there's nothing new for us about measuring what each and every employee achieves in relation to agreed targets of efficiency or achievement. The session I went to offered the opportunity to examine alternative ways of going about it, and it was as useful as it promised to be. In the spirit of consultation, I've presented all the options on the intranet, so people can look at it and then we'll have a discussion phase. I hope it'll work out, because I don't want everyone to feel any new system is imposed from above.

[pause]

Now listen to the recording again.

[pause]

That is the end of Part Two.

Part Three. Questions 23 to 30.

You will hear a discussion between two business journalists, Nick and Rachel, who are going to write a review of a book about career planning.

For each question, 23–30, mark one letter (A, B or C) for the correct answer.

After you have listened once, replay the recording.

You now have 45 seconds to read through the questions.

[pause]

Now listen, and mark A, B or C.

[pause]

Man: Which of the new titles shall we start with, Rachel?
Woman: I don't know about you Nick, but I've got most to say about *The Career Adventurer*.
Man: The latest volume by Karen Ward. Yes, we could make that the title of our feature.
Woman: Absolutely, and the first thing worth commenting on is the catchy title. It immediately grabs the attention.
Man: It's not as if you can get many thrills once you actually get beyond the front cover though. It's basically a workmanlike, step-by-step guide to career planning.
Woman: At least it's a much lighter read than other volumes on career planning.
Man: Fair point. But there was certainly a mismatch between the initial expectations I had that were raised by the title, and what you actually get when you start reading.
Woman: Yeah, yeah, I wouldn't disagree with that but I felt there were other greater letdowns in the book . . . like the advice sections at the end of chapters.
Man: Go on.
Woman: Well, each chapter starts OK . . . the first one on recruitment methods is potentially useful . . . and there are noteworthy quotes in the case studies. And as I read each chapter I was expecting it to culminate in some real insight . . . and the advice pages were quite interesting I suppose. But I was still left feeling dissatisfied. The author tells us she's racked up a series of mini-careers, and this does nothing to lend credibility to her words. The more I ploughed through her words of wisdom, the more I wondered is this really what she could have learnt about advanced resumé writing and career burnout while working as an accounts clerk or whatever?
Man: That's interesting. She's had a few books published, including the trio on successful entrepreneurs we featured a while ago, and I think they kind of give the impression that her connection with the world of business is tenuous. I don't think that should take anything away from this latest volume though. I mean, it's a very useful digest of existing pieces about the workplace which you'd have to really trawl the internet and self-help books to find out about.
Woman: Absolutely.
Man: You mentioned the opening section on recruitment methods. Was there anything else in the book you think our readers would find particularly helpful?
Woman: Helpful . . . um, I know what I found highly readable. In the second chapter a careers adviser talks about embarrassing blunders, gaffes people make when they're under pressure during interviews or haven't prepared for the occasion. Some of it's very funny and comes as a welcome relief after the long-winded section on applying for positions.
Man: Mm, guaranteed to raise a few smiles. Especially for anyone who's been around for a while or has ever had a similar experience.
Woman: Oh but – and this is a criticism of the whole book – I think that it feels oddly old-fashioned. I mean it addresses the subject of work in the context of traditional employment, and makes an assumption that people consider anything less than full-time employment only when they're nearing retirement.
Man: Yes, and there was that study recently about people in the thirty to forty age range who are experiencing more and more that a portfolio career is the norm. And the book simply fails to address this.
Woman: Exactly.
Man: It does offer valuable suggestions for finding the right employer for you, and how to get ahead in your career.
Woman: It says the key thing is finding something you enjoy doing, which I'd go along with of course. I did think the author made an error of judgement in reproducing the *Strong Interest Inventory* for readers to try out. That was the test developed at Stanford in the nineteen twenties. What I call the 'magazine test' is infinitely simpler.
Man: Oh what's that?

Key

Woman: You think what magazine you're most likely to buy, and find a job in that field. You'll love it so much you're bound to be successful.
Man: Right. Do you agree the paltry fourteen pounds ninety-nine is a very reasonable price?
Woman: It's not paltry if you're a student or aren't in work . . . although it isn't so dear as to price students out of the market completely. And, unlike a lot of books of this type, it doesn't try to command a higher price by purporting to be an academic volume.
Man: True.
Woman: Would you buy it?
Man: Erm . . . it's difficult . . . I've had to sit down and read the thing from cover to cover in a day, so my judgement's clouded. For me, this falls into the 'of minor interest' category, and it's saved only by the well-chosen case studies, which I suspect people will skip over most of each chapter to get to.
Woman: Possibly. Now, shall we . . .

[pause]

Now listen to the recording again.

[pause]

That is the end of Part Three. You now have ten minutes to transfer your answers to your Answer Sheet.

[pause]

Note: Teacher, stop the recording here and time ten minutes. Remind students when there is **one** minute remaining.

That is the end of the test.

Test 3   Reading

Part 1

1 C   2 E   3 D   4 B   5 C   6 D   7 A   8 B

Part 2

9 C   10 A   11 B   12 G   13 D   14 E

Part 3

15 D   16 A   17 B   18 C   19 A   20 B

Part 4

21 D   22 A   23 A   24 C   25 D   26 B   27 C   28 D   29 B   30 A

Part 5

31 IT   32 WITH   33 ALTHOUGH / THOUGH / WHILE / WHILST   34 WHAT
35 BE   36 MY   37 FOR   38 TAKE   39 TO   40 WHICH

Part 6

41 THE   42 SUCH   43 CORRECT   44 WELL   45 BUT   46 CORRECT
47 ALL   48 THIS   49 HOW   50 SO   51 OF   52 IF

Test 3 Writing

Question 1
Sample A

> Introduction
> The aim of this report is to describe and compare the average numbers of conference attendees in three categories, which are individuals, small companies and large organisations. The observed conferences are "Successful Communication", "Internet Selling" and "Marketing Today".
>
> Successful Communication
> To start with successful communication, the bar chart represents that 50 individuals and 60 visitors from small companies attended this conference, whereas 120 people were from a large organisation.
>
> Internet Selling
> We can see that this conference was mostly visited by individuals with 100 people, followed by visitors from small companies. However, the smallest group of visitors were people from large organisations with a number of 60.
>
> Marketing Today
> The bar chart shows that there was a good mix of visitors. There were 80 individuals, followed by 90 people from large organisations. However, the best group were visitors from small companies with totally 100 people.
>
> To sum up, individuals were mostly interested in internet selling, whereas people from small companies mostly attended marketing today. However, staff from large organisations preferred the conference "Successful Communication".

Scales	Mark	Commentary
Content	4	All the content is relevant to the task and the target reader would be on the whole informed.
Communicative Achievement	3	Uses the conventions of a report effectively with a clear purpose stated which holds the target reader's attention (*the aim to this report is to describe and compare*). The report communicates the ideas clearly and the register is consistently appropriate.
Organisation	4	The text is generally well-organised and coherent. A number of headings help the organisation of the report and linking words are used effectively (*to start with, to sum up, however, whereas*).
Language	3	The report uses vocabulary relevant to the topic and simple grammatical structures generally appropriately. There are occasional errors, but these are non-impeding (*with totally 100 people*).

Key

Sample B

> ATTENDANCE PATTERNS AT 3 CONFERENCES.
>
> SUMMARY
>
> This report shows and comments on the attendance patterns at three conferences run by the Central Business Centre (C.B.C.), focusing on how to effectively advertise next events to potential attendees.
>
> INTRODUCTION
>
> The C.B.C. wishes to investigate how the attendance to their conferences is split in terms of people either working for small/large companies or attending on an individual basis. This will help them tailor the advertisement of new conferences.
>
> OBSERVATIONS
>
> By ranking the conferences per overall attendance:
>
> Marketing today: 270
> Internet Selling: 250
> Communication: 230
>
> marketing is found to be the most appealing topic.
>
> However, looking at the split into the 3 attendee subjects, Communication Skills, looks particularly important for people working for large companies.
>
> CONCLUSION.
>
> We recommend advertising future conferences on Communication through direct contact with Human Resources Department of large companies.

Scales	Mark	Commentary
Content	1	The main content points are not covered. Only the totals of attendees at each conference are given. The target reader would be minimally informed.
Communicative Achievement	2	The report communicates simple ideas with some control. The register is consistently appropriate.
Organisation	2	The text is organised by headings although *'conclusion'* is inappropriate. Some substitution and linking words are used effectively (*them* for *the Central Business Centre* and *however*). The main body of the section *'observations'* is bullet points and this would only be appropriate to this task if the totals were deemed relevant.
Language	3	Everyday vocabulary is used appropriately (*tailor the advertisement, particularly important for*). A range of grammatical forms are used with control (*this will help them tailor*).

Question 2
Sample C

> We are going to Lose one of our Biggest Customer
>
> Introduction
>
> The aim of this report is to analyse the current situation with the danger of losing one of our biggest customer and give some reasons why this has happened. The report also includes recommendations to deal with this situation.
>
> Reasons for the Situation
>
> The reasons for this situation seem to be heavy. We had been asked for claryfication and rather we went to the chairman of the company to ask some questions. What we found was that competitors offered better conditions as we did. This can be attributed to the fact that the quality of the products is different.
>
> Moreover, the particular customer has had delivery problems and trubles with the service. This referers to a weak experience in the past and it seems unlikely for the convidence between business partners. We therefore have to find a solution how to improve the relationship for the future.
>
> Recommendations
>
> The competition in this sector is strong. We should therefore consider a special training in providing the company and its service. In addition, we should make an annual survey with customers to see how satisfied they are with our current service. To summarize I think that the future prospects are promising.
>
> Your comments on the above report would be very welcome.

Scales	Mark	Commentary
Content	2	All the content points are addressed, but not entirely successfully. Content point 3 is unclear (*a special training in providing the company and its service*). The target reader would not be fully informed.
Communicative Achievement	2	Uses the convention of the task to communicate straightforward ideas in a generally appropriate way to hold the target reader's attention.
Organisation	3	The report opens with a clear reason for writing. The text is organised with suitable headings and uses a range of linking words (*moreover, in addition, to summarize*).
Language	1	A number of errors are present (*better conditions as we did, rather we went to the chairman*) which distract the target reader and impede communication. There are spelling slips with everyday vocabulary (*claryfication, trubles, convidence*).

Key

Sample D

> Report on change in customers purchasing behavior
>
> This report aims to outline the reasons for one of our biggest customers to drift orders away from our company to a competitor. Moreover, the report seeks to present possible solutions on how to resolve the situation and regain the investor's confidence.
>
> As a starting point of this report the reasons for the customers' behavior were analyzed. The investigation &unknown; the evolution of the customers ordering behavior by looking at past orders, talking to our &unknown; relationship manager, interviewing other suppliers and utilyizing our firm's network to understand what our competitor does better than us.
>
> The findings of the investigation were twofold. Firstly, our competitor's reach &unknown; to client orders is later than ours. Conversations with industry specialists revealed that our order automation system is dated compared to our competitors.
>
> Secondly, our competitor can add additional value to the client through better &unknown; management. Although subjective, our due diligence showed that our competitor can predict more customer tailored solutions than we can.
>
> The solutions that present themselves from the above ellaborated points are the following: A task force with the goal to close the technological gap should be created. Secondly, we will contract a head hunter to select and propose a relationship manager from our competition who is in a position to fullfill our clients needs. The goal is to subsequently permit our actions taken to the customer.
>
> In conclusion, we identified &unknown; in our order automation system as well as relationship management. To address there shortfalls we suggest to creat an IT taskforce and contract a head hunter to select an appropriate relationship manager.

Scales	Mark	Commentary
Content	4	All content is relevant and the points are expanded. The target reader would be informed.
Communicative Achievement	4	Uses the convention of a report effectively with a clear purpose (*this report aims to outline the reasons and to address there shortfalls*) and a conclusion (although this is not a requirement of the task). These hold the target reader's attention. The report communicates the ideas clearly and the register is appropriately formal.
Organisation	4	Uses clear paragraphing to deal with each content point and organise the ideas effectively and communicate the ideas well. The sentences are very effectively linked (*As a starting point, firstly, secondly, in conclusion*).
Language	4	The report uses a relatively wide range of appropriate vocabulary and complex grammar forms with control (*Although subjective, our due diligence showed that our competitor can predict more customer tailored solutions than we can*).

Question 3
Sample E

> Dear Sir/Madam
>
> We are writing to complain about your recent article, released on April 10, concerning our company. In our view, the article was disappointing because of the mistakes it contained, which we mention in the next paragraph. Afterwards, we would like to give you our opinion concerning those misleadings. Last but not least, some recommendations to correct the errors.
>
> First of all, we would like to outline the wrong informations you wrote in your article which were the sales figures, the environmental protection, the outlook and the redundancies.
>
> The article reports about a decrease in our sales. However, our Chairman during his last conference said that the sales doubled. What is more, the article mentioned a non-environmental protection from our enterprise, which is disappointing because we have been taking care about this topic, in fact, we recycle almost all our materials and have recently installed solar panels in our factories.
>
> Nevertheless, our perspectives are optimistic and not negative as stated in the article. Moreover, we are going to expand our business, opening two new warehouses and recruiting new staff and not, as you wrote, make redundant people.
>
> Finally, we hope that the article will be rettified because of the reasons mentioned before.
>
> We are looking forward to receiving from you also a letter of excuses.
>
> Yours faithfully

Scales	Mark	Commentary
Content	3	All the content points are covered and the target reader would be informed. However, the third content point is not appropriately expanded upon and the first content point is dealt with in a cursory way.
Communicative Achievement	3	The letter communicates the message to the target reader effectively with appropriate register and tone (*we are writing to complain about your recent article*).
Organisation	4	The text is well organised with an appropriate opening and closing. A number of linking words are used effectively (*first of all, however, nevertheless, moreover and finally*).
Language	3	The letter uses a range of vocabulary although the choice of vocabulary is not always successful (*misleadings, letter of excuses*). A range of simple grammatical structures are used with a good degree of control (*first of all, we would like to outline the wrong informations you wrote in your article*). Errors are present, but do not impede communication.

Key

Sample F

> Dear Sir and Madam,
>
> With refrence to your published article in the international business magazine of 2nd June, I am writing to express my desegreement on some statements made. I have to point out:
>
> First point we have an excellent communication sistem and not as you wrote a caothic sistem to communicate with out employees.
>
> We have all importent figures and dates on the intranet. There is also the feasability to look up the birthdays of our employees or training programm which are available.
>
> Second point is the low pay for our employees and in addition to that you assume that the long working hours are illigel.
>
> I have to regret these points. Our Human Resources Department is alway controlling these
>
> However my souggestie is that you come to visit our company so you will have the possibility to make some interview.
>
> You will write a new article in which you point out the wrong statments If it well not be reprinted we will have to take legal action.
>
> I look forward to hearing from you in due course.
>
> Yours faithfully

Scales	Mark	Commentary
Content	2	Point 2 is inadequately addressed as it does not present a detailed defence (*Our Human Resources Department is always controlling these*) so the target reader would not be fully informed.
Communicative Achievement	2	The letter uses the conventions of the task to communicate ideas in a generally appropriate way.
Organisation	2	The letter uses some linking words (*however, in addition*). However, the paragraphing is weak as most of the paragraphs are single sentences. The opening and closing formulae are correct.
Language	1	Noticeable errors are present with the spelling of common words (*refence, desegreement, importent, illigel*). The letter uses a limited range of simple structures which are not always entirely successful (*If it well now be reprinted*). The grammatical errors would distract and confuse the target reader (*I have to regret these points*).

Question 4

Sample G

Proposal for a new marketing strategy

Introduction

This proposal suggests some ideas for revision of our current marketing strategy, with the aim to boost our company's sales.

Findings

The fact that our sales have fallen significantly over the last three monts requires an urgent action. Our sales team has already taken some measures: at the start of March, when noticed first signs of falling, they gave a discount to some categories of customers, especially the ones higly affected by the curent economic crisis. However, that has not given any result yet.

However, the current situation is not the only factor causing the fail. Our marketing strategy also has to be considered and adjusted to the changed conditions. When we defined it, during the 2009 Business plan preparation (which was last summer), the market research done by our leading agency of such type indicated a need for premium products development. This is why we targeted new consumer groups, i.e. ones with high income, and all the consequent marketing activities aimed to attract this specific group.

According to my opinion, the current marketing strategy does not fit with the current situation.

Recommendation

We should organize a new market research, which woud give us an idea on our customers' and consumers' needs in this particular moment. There are strong indications that the picture will significanty differ from the previous one, i.e. that they would rather go for cheaper products: The next phase would be to start with multiple promotions, targeted to different groups of consumers, e.g. children, students, etc. We should employ TV advertising as a main channel, since it is the most popular one. In addition with that, promotion-related events should be organized in all bigger cities. I recommend also our presence at concerts and music shows.

CONCLUSION

In conclusion, there is a need to revise our marketing strategy towards "value" products. That would at least keep our sales volume at the same level, of course if we support the process effectively. In addition, we will enhance our public image by better understanding of our consumers' concerns.

For that reason, I strongly recommend to implement the changes as soon as possible.

Key

Scales	Mark	Commentary
Content	3	All the content points are addressed. However, the answer does not clearly explain what is wrong with the strategy; it is more a description of it. Also, the second and third content points are underdeveloped.
Communicative Achievement	3	The proposal communicates the message and would hold the target reader's attention. The register and tone are appropriate throughout.
Organisation	4	The proposal is well-organised with a title and appropriate headings and effective use of cohesive devices and substitution (*they* for *sales team*, *that* for *discount*, *it* for *marketing strategy*, *however*).
Language	4	The text uses a range of relevant vocabulary and collocation (*fallen significantly*, *strong indications*). It uses a wide range of simple and complex grammatical forms with good control (*The next phase would be to start with multiple promotions*).

Sample H

PROPOSAL FOR NEW MARKETING STRATEGY

Purpose

The aim of this proposal is to suggest new marketing strategies in order to change the current bad situation.

Current Strategy

At present, we are loosing plenty of accounts. The current economical situation is one of the culprits, but other reasons are involved. Our products are for a specialized type of customer, between 60 and 75, who has a lot of experience and information about the product. However, our last advertising campaigns are being focused on the whole market, without taking this segment of the market into account.

New strategy

It would be interesting to appear on the most important specialized magazine in the sector, "Media", so that we reach this target customer.

Apart from this, an important advertising campaign would be carried out on TV, led to people between 60 and 75. The main reasons for this change of strategy are that lots of hours are spent in front of TV by this kind of customer. Furthermore, since they have a lot of free time, they like to read specialized magazines about products like ours to keep informed and compare prices.

Recommendations

This strategy would allow us reach our target customer and, as a consequence, improve sales. I therefore recommend we proceed with it.

Scales	Mark	Commentary
Content	3	All content points are addressed and the target reader is on the whole informed.
Communicative Achievement	2	The conventions for the communicative task are generally used appropriately and the proposal communicates simple straightforward ideas.
Organisation	3	The proposal is organised with suitable headings and a clear purpose (*The aim of this proposal is to suggest new marketing strategies to communicate straightforward ideas*). Also, cohesive devices are used relatively well.
Language	2	Errors are noticeable and sometimes distracting. Spelling is variable (*loosing plenty, recomend* are incorrect, but *campaign* is correct). However, in general, errors do not impede communication (*appear on a magazine*).

Test 3 Listening

Part 1

1 (A) CAMCORDER / VIDEO CAMERA
2 (THE) OHP(S)
3 CASE STUDIES / CASE STUDY (MATERIALS / PAPERS / DOCUMENTS
4 BENEFITS FROM / OF COACHING
5 PHYSICAL FITNESS
6 TEAM MOTIVATION
7 PERFORMANCE IMPROVEMENT
8 NEGOTIATING / NEGOTIATION STRATEGIES
9 TROUBLE(-)SHOOTING
10 MANAGEMENT MODELS
11 SUCCESSION PLANNING
12 (THE / A) KEYNOTE SPEECH

Part 2

13 G   14 B   15 E   16 A   17 D   18 D   19 C   20 G   21 E   22 B

Part 3

23 C   24 A   25 B   26 B   27 A   28 C   29 A   30 C

Tapescript

Listening Test 3

This is the Business English Certificate Higher 5, Listening Test 3.

Part One. Questions 1 to 12.

You will hear a recording that a training manager has made for his assistant, describing plans for a training day that he will be running with his colleague, Julia.

As you listen, for questions 1 to 12, complete the notes, using up to three words or a number.

Key

After you have listened once, replay the recording.

You now have 45 seconds to read through the notes.

[pause]

Now listen, and complete the notes.

[pause]

I hope you don't mind me leaving a recording, but something has cropped up and Julia and I have had to go off to head office, so we can't speak to you in person. We've finalised our plans for the management training day we're putting on for Standford's on the seventeenth of next month, so could you take the necessary action, please.

The most urgent thing is to contact the venue, that's the Swan Hotel, and get them to provide a camcorder as well as the video recorder and TV we've already booked, as ours isn't working and I don't think we can get it fixed in time. And at the same time, because we've rethought how to run the first workshop, we won't be needing the OHPs after all, so you might as well cancel those.

Oh, and when you send the programme to the participants, could you point out that the case study we've already circulated to them is for the discussion slot: otherwise I'm sure half of them will forget to take it with them.

Then you'd better ring Standford's, and tell them that the guest speaker has agreed to change her topic to 'Benefits from coaching': we managed to persuade her that 'Financial instruments' would be too heavy for the end of the day!

Right, now we've finalised the programme, so could you get it typed up? Here's the running order. It's a nine o'clock start and naturally, we'll introduce ourselves and outline the programme. It'll be a good idea for us to make everybody really alert as a priority, so at nine fifteen we're starting with my talk on physical fitness, which is about its importance at work. The payoff is that Julia can take over at ten and do her session on team motivation – that'll be a workshop format.

Now that'll take us to a mid-morning break at ten forty-five. I don't think they should have too long, as we don't want to lose momentum. The obvious thing to follow the break is the discussion session, which we're calling 'Performance Improvement', because it's an extension and application of what Julia will have been talking about before the coffee break, and should provide food for thought. By the time that's over, at twelve o'clock, some of them will be beginning to lose concentration before lunch, and we should end the morning with a role play. This went so well last time. It'll be focusing on negotiating strategies. It should make an interesting session.

I think that'll leave them in a positive frame of mind for lunch at about one. Julia will start the afternoon at two with her session on troubleshooting. I'm sure participants will come up with plenty of questions about that. Then at three fifteen, we've got the two parallel sessions.

They can choose the presentation 'Management Models', which will be aimed mostly at the less experienced participants, but there'll be a workshop at the same time on 'Succession Planning', which might appeal mostly to more senior managers. It's something that too few companies think about until it's too late. Then at four o'clock, we'll bring everyone together for the keynote speech. We thought of setting aside a time for questions and answers, but quite honestly they've got most of the day for that, so we won't bother.

OK, that's all, so if you could deal with that today or tomorrow, I'd be most grateful.

[pause]

Now listen to the recording again.

[pause]

That is the end of Part One. You now have 20 seconds to check your answers.

[pause]

Part Two. Questions 13 to 22.

Test 3

You will hear five different people talking about the issues involved in having new buildings constructed.

For each extract there are two tasks. Look at Task One. For each question, 13 to 17, decide what problem occurred with the construction project, from the list A–H. Now look at Task Two. For each question, 18–22, choose what advice about new construction projects each speaker gives, from the list A–H.

After you have listened once, replay the recording.

You now have 30 seconds to read the two lists.

[pause]

Now listen, and do the two tasks.

[pause]

Speaker One

Man: We decided to open this new production facility on the outskirts of Madrid. I think we felt that the location was not too difficult to commute to, space not a problem, etc. The proposal was well within budget, so we didn't spot the fact that the necessary link road wasn't included in the developer's original outline. The problem was fixed, but completing on time was very tight – we nearly missed the opening. I think with hindsight I'd say that once you've sorted out your contractors, it's worth making a small internal group responsible for overseeing things so somebody is looking at the detail. And this pays off even if they have to put aside their own work for a while.

Speaker Two

Woman: Things never turn out as planned when you're looking at building. Costs always overrun, so we thought we were very smart in keeping a tight rein on the contractors. This focus on the site meant the manager responsible for internal fixtures, etc was on his own and went way over budget. It'll take us a while to recoup this and, as you can imagine, he's not very happy at the moment. Still, it's a lesson. I think I'd recommend that this is not handled internally and that, even for smaller parts of the contract, it's worth getting a range of companies to put in a bid. They, and you, are then tied to the best deal and your staff are not tested beyond their abilities!

Speaker Three

Man: There are always technical problems when you're building on a new site – we couldn't even get onto the site in the first week because the access hadn't been finished on time. But it's the ongoing problems that prevent it being a success such as new equipment constantly breaking down or, as in our case, a faulty ventilation system, which now needs replacing. In future, I would make sure I'd checked out whoever was fitting it with their previous customers. I think it's important to give them targets of certain standards you want them to fulfil throughout the process. Perhaps it's also worth getting a fairly senior member of staff to check up on these contractors.

Speaker Four

Woman: I have to say that when we built the new site in the Aosta valley the route in was very steep and we thought parking would be an issue – it was a big facility with lots of staff. We didn't foresee that worrying about that would mean that the construction work fell behind and the contractors didn't meet one of their interim deadlines. Fortunately, we still managed to control the costs. But it's a learning curve and if we did it again, I think we could look into what other options were possible. We were offered what looked like a good deal, and we took it without really considering all the possibilities that the consultants on the project had suggested.

133

Key

Speaker Five

Man: When you're expanding onto a new site, I think it's important to make sure the schedule is realistic. We really rushed through the various completion stages and prided ourselves on reaching all our targets. But this meant certain things were overlooked and we suffered a series of problems in the first few months the facility was open. We sent very few managers to the site as there wasn't much space for them and that meant there weren't enough people around to arrange the necessary checks on the machinery that kept the whole site operational. Certainly, I would recommend that several different options are considered when you're arranging after-sales contracts. Make it competitive and make sure you get one that includes regular checks.

[pause]

Now listen to the recording again.

[pause]

That is the end of Part Two.

[pause]

Part Three. Questions 23 to 30.

You will hear a meeting involving members of a quality improvement group in a manufacturing company. The department head, Sandra, is talking to a female colleague, Fiona, and a male colleague, Jamie.

For each question, 23-30, mark one letter (A, B or C) for the correct answer.

After you have listened once, replay the recording.

You have 45 seconds to read through the questions.

[pause]

Now listen, and mark A, B or C.

[pause]

Woman:	Have you got the list of topics I circulated?
Man:	Mmn.
Woman:	Right. First, the perennial problem of telephone calls.
Man:	Yes. It's so irritating when someone's phone is left ringing because they're away from their desk.
Woman:	It's ages before anyone bothers to answer the phone for them.
Woman:	Isn't the real reason that often callers ask for somebody they've spoken to before, but it may be a completely different matter, which that person can't deal with? And we're so used to that happening, we're not taking calls seriously.
Man:	Then callers get annoyed that we can't help them.
Woman:	Right.
Woman:	Shall we get the switchboard to ask what they're ringing about?
Man, Woman:	Yes.
Woman:	But shouldn't we also set a time limit for answering the phone?
Woman:	Perhaps we could measure the time people take to answer, and see if there really is a problem.
Woman:	But we mustn't tell everyone, or they'll answer quickly, and it won't be realistic.
Man:	What about some training?
Woman:	No, maybe Fiona's right, her idea is all we need. And we can repeat the exercise in six months' time.

Man:	OK.
Woman:	Next there's sales. We all know there's a slowdown, but we don't seem to be responding adequately.
Man:	I reckon we ought to use the internet more actively. Our website brings in a trickle of customers, but we need to benchmark by looking at other companies' sites, too.
Woman:	To see how our products stand up to comparison?
Man:	Right. Our customers could be buying from anywhere in the world. We don't really know enough about how we compare in price, or quality.
Woman:	It probably wouldn't help sales directly. What else could we do?
Woman:	What about discounts, to encourage customers to purchase larger quantities?
Man:	Our products aren't really price-sensitive. Customers buy them for quality and reliability.
Woman:	Then they're the selling points we should be publicising.
Man:	The effect would be marginal. But if we broadened our range, customers could purchase goods from us that they currently source from other suppliers.
Woman:	Good idea. Fiona?
Woman:	Yes.
Woman:	Then we'll look into that in depth next time. Next, we need more support staff, so sales people can spend more time selling. What do you think?
Woman:	Yes, ideally. But we'll never get an increase in staffing levels though.
Man:	You're right. There's already a policy of cuts through natural wastage. There's no point trying to change it.
Woman:	You know Sarah, in Accounts? She wants a new job, and she's too good to lose. Maybe she could be transferred.
Woman:	And Accounts have just upgraded their software, so they probably don't need all their staff.
Man:	There might be other people too.
Woman:	Then let's propose that. Now shifts. You wanted to raise this, Fiona?
Woman:	Oh yes. The Quality Control records show that since the night shift was introduced, it's had a very high percentage of defective items that have to be rejected. We need to reduce the figure.
Man:	I think it's because some people who used to work only on day shifts don't like working at night.
Woman:	Yes, several supervisors have noticed the resentment. I think it'll die down of its own accord. But Fiona, the problem you mentioned is normal with night shifts. We can't do much about it.
Woman:	At least we should look into it.
Man:	I agree.
Woman:	OK. Next time then. Now Jamie, you wanted to bring up communication.
Man:	Yes. I know that senior management takes communication very seriously, and encourages things like phoning and emailing customers to get feedback on products, and using the intranet so all the staff know about vacancies, new policies, and so on. But some basic things aren't adequately dealt with. The purchasing officers are always complaining that it's too long before they're told about sales orders.
Woman:	It would help if we had a communications officer.
Woman:	But *we* can suggest improvements to any of the departmental heads.
Man:	I agree with Fiona. If a position is created with that particular responsibility, it signals that communication *is* taken seriously.
Woman:	Well the company *does* take it seriously. So if we don't signal that ourselves, maybe we should propose that one of the senior managers takes it on.
Woman:	It's worth trying.
Man:	Yes.
Woman:	Right. Well that's everything for today. Thank you both very much.

[pause]

Now listen to the recording again.

[pause]

Key

That is the end of Part Three. You now have ten minutes to transfer your answers to your Answer Sheet.
[pause]

Note: Teacher, stop the recording and time ten minutes. Remind students when there is **one** minute remaining.

That is the end of the test.

Test 4 Reading

Part 1

1 C   2 E   3 A   4 B   5 C   6 D   7 A   8 B

Part 2

9 E   10 D   11 G   12 A   13 F   14 C

Part 3

15 D   16 A   17 C   18 B   19 C   20 B

Part 4

21 D   22 B   23 A   24 D   25 A   26 C   27 D   28 B   29 A   30 C

Part 5

31 WHOSE   32 OUT   33 IN   34 NOW   35 FOR   36 NOT   37 AND
38 SO   39 TO   40 THAT

Part 6

41 WHERE   42 CORRECT   43 CORRECT   44 WAS   45 CORRECT
46 TAKEN   47 ON   48 DO   49 THE   50 WITH   51 UP   52 ABOUT

Test 4 Writing

Question 1

Sample A

> Report: Enrolments Prediction For The 3 Courses In Next Year
>
> Location: Wakeley Business College
>
> Effective Management: Generally speaking the predicted number of participants fluctates in the next year. In spring session, the number is the lowest, which is only 50. Then it reaches the peak of 80 in both summer and autumn session. At last it drops to 80 in winter.

Customer Communications: The number change chart is different with that of effective management. In spring it is 60 and drops to 50 in summer, which is same with in autumn. Then, it reaches the peak of 90 in winter.

Marketing in Practice: As the change of the course of customer communication, the numbers in spring and winter are larger than in summer and autumn. It reaches the peak of 120 in spring, then drops sharply to only 70 in summer. But in autumn and winter, it increases steadily, which is 80 and 100 respectively.

Conclusion: marketing in practice may be the most popular course of the largest number of predicted paticipants, especially in Spring and Winter. Fewest students are thought to participate in the course of customer communications especially in summer and autumn.

Scales	Mark	Commentary
Content	4	All the content is addressed with some expansion and relevant comparison between the different courses (*marketing in practice may be the most popular course of the largest number of predicted participants*). The target reader would be fully informed.
Communicative Achievement	3	The conventions of the communicative task are used to hold the target reader's attention and communicate straightforward ideas.
Organisation	3	The report is connected and coherent using each course as a heading. Some cohesive devices and linking are used effectively (*which* and *it* for *numbers of participants*, *but*).
Language	3	Appropriate language for making comparisons is used to good effect (*fluctuates, reaches the peak, the most popular, drops sharply*). Errors with articles and prepositions are present (*chart is different with*), but the meaning can still be determined.

Sample B

Introduction

The report is set out to predict enrolments for the Wakeley Business College's three courses for the next year base on the survey from (next) last year.

Findings

Take look at the bar chart we could find that the Effective Mangement class figure is the lowest only about 50 people. Then grow up as twice by Summer and Autumn then slide down to 60 at winter. The Customer Communications

Key

> class's enrolments at spring was 60 then slide down to 50 get back to 90 in the end. The participants on Marketing in Practice class in spring is twice as customer communication course as 120 the fall down to 100 by winter.
>
> Conclusion
>
> As we can see, the three course's participants all fluctuated slightly in last year. But the numbers of participants on marketing in Practice was always more than two of other courses.
>
> Recommendation
>
> Since figure on participants on Customer Communications and Marketing in practice was on a upward trend. We suggested that Wakeley Business College offere more times on this two courses and the mean time encourage people paticipate the other course.

Scales	Mark	Commentary
Content	2	All the bar charts are referred to with limited expansion. The information for the Effective Management course is not entirely accurate (*then grow up as twice by Summer and Autumn*). Also, the information on Marketing in Practice is incomplete. The target reader would only be partially informed.
Communicative Achievement	2	The report uses the convention of the communicative task to hold the target reader's attention. The register is generally appropriate but not always consistent (*take look at the bar chart*).
Organisation	2	The text is coherent and connected using appropriate headings and simple linking words (*but, and*).
Language	2	A range of simple grammatical forms are used with some control although the courses are referred to in both the past and present tense. Also, the language used to describe movement is inaccurate (*grow up, slide down*). However, appropriate vocabulary for comparisons is used effectively (*the lowest, fluctuated, upward trend*).

Question 2
Sample C

> Report on the possible effects of a competitor on our retail outlet
>
> Introduction
>
> In response to a request from our line manager I would like to submit the following report which aims to analyze the possible effects of a newly opened store nearby on our own retail outlet which has been running successfully.

The Target Customer of the Competitor

Similar to our own store, the competitor's new store positions its prospective consumer among the middle-class people, that is to say, those people whose income is the medium lever, especially those middle-aged people who hold a post in companies. Undoubtedly, their target consumers do not differ much from our company, hwihc has been enjoying its prestige in the cell-phone sales industry.

Possible Effects brought on our store

Through the long-term observation and research by our staff, we have found that a substantial number of our old customers have turned to the new store away from ours. This can be attributed to the fact that the new store has been implementing the 'price penetration' strategy since it opened esp. as well as that the cell-phones they provide are of high quality and unique style, according to the survey conducted among customers who have shifted their attention away from our store. Tehrefore, it can be easily predicted that if no immediate measures are taken, the side-effect on tour outlet will deteriorate. Moreover, the existing customers will be less interested in our product, and iit will be more difficult for us to expand our customer base.

Measures that can be Taken

Faced such situation, the best way to regain customers' trust and interst on our cell-phone products is to pay more attention to the innovation and development of our product so as to further enhance the quality of our products. In this way, can we attract a larger number of customers.

Furthermore, the after-sale service of our store could be further improved. For instance, we can give better warranty of the cell-phone we provides and better maintainence and tuition service of the products. In a word, to best serve customers' needs and offer impeccable service is the key to our business success.

Scales	Mark	Commentary
Content	5	All the content points are relevant and expanded effectively. The target reader would be fully informed.
Communicative Achievement	4	The ideas are communicated in an appropriate register and tone which hold the target reader's attention throughout the report. It communicates complex and straightforward ideas effectively.
Organisation	4	The report is well-organised with an early reference to the reason for writing (*In response to a request from our line manager … which aims to analyse the possible effects*). It also uses headings which help the overall organisation. Cohesive devices and linking words are used to good effect (*who* for *people*, *this* for *action of turning to new store, furthermore, therefore*).
Language	4	A wide range of vocabulary and complex forms are used with good control (*This can be attributed to the facts that the new store has been implementing the price penetration strategy*). Occasional errors are present (*turned to the new store away from ours*), but these do not impede communication.

Sample D

Introduction and Background

Further to the phone conversation of yesterday, I was writing to detail the things related to our company's competitors; new store. To begin with I would like to outline what the situation was and what has changed concerning the new store previously led by our most successful retail outlet, all the surrounding small shops take only a slice of pizza in the retail sector in city centre. It appeared that no one would be able to change that until our strongest rival, the Wu-Mart established the aggressive plan to open a new store not far away from ours. It take no doubt terribly negative impact on our future sales when its cost advantage was concerned, therefore, some measures should be taken to win this competition.

Customer and Market

Things seemed to be not bad if Wu-Mart just take greater interested in sport cloth, which definitely can only catch the eyes the people aged from 10 to 40. In China, the number of people who take great passion for sport is limitation. In other words, there was a difference between our company and Wu-mart in target custom. As a successful retail outlet we aim to provide the service to all the people for their necessary demant on a daily basis, fortunately. Our rival apparently didn't.

In future

I think the above should be given a high priority because the employee tend to feel insecured and lost if they can't see it clearly. In sport cloth area, we are supposed to better our source and do our best to offer a lower price, which would naturely increase our marketshare and power our competition ability...for more detail, please refer to my attachments.

To be continued.

Scales	Mark	Commentary
Content	2	Content point 1 is only partially addressed as it is unclear who is being targeted. Content point 2 lacks expansion (*terribly negative impact on our future sales*). The target reader would not be fully informed.
Communicative Achievement	2	Straightforward ideas are communicated using the conventions of the task although the register is not always entirely appropriate (*to be continued, things seemed to be not bad*).
Organisation	3	The text is generally well organised and uses headings. Cohesive devices (*when, which, who*) are generally used to good effect.
Language	1	Errors are frequent and distracting. The meaning in parts is unclear and impedes communication (*it take no doubt terribly negative impact, in sport cloth we are supposed to better our source*).

Question 3

Sample E

Dear Sir/Madam,

We are writing to express our interest in a market research report for Latin America where we would like to expand to.

Our bank, XYZ AG, is not only well established in our home country in Switzerland but also in Asia where we expanded our business to ten years ago. Our core business is the wealth management for private clients who are living there.

Last month we have decided that would like to expand into Latin America where we see a huge potential. Therefore we would need a market research report. This report should consist of the following points:

- Where do the most wealthy Latin American people live?
- Would these people consider opening an account with a foreign bank like XYZ and what service would they require?
- Would they prefer to be advised from our staff in Swtizerland or would they like to have an advisory office in their home country?

Having this market research report containing the information mentioned-above we would decide if we are going to open an advisory office in Latin America and where. Additionally, we would be able to prepare our advisors for their new duties.

If you are interested in providing us with this report please send an email or letter within the next ten days to the address mentioned-below with a proposal of how the report would look like and the conditions of your company.

We look forward to hearing from you.

Yours faithfully,

AAA BBBB   Peter Miller

Project Manager   Deskhead Project Management Lat Am

XYZ AG

P.O. BOX 5000

5055 Basel, Switzerland

aaaa.bbbb@xyz.com

Key

Scales	Mark	Commentary
Content	5	All the content is relevant to the task and the target reader would be fully informed.
Communicative Achievement	4	The letter holds the target reader's attention with a clear purpose stated for writing (*We are writing to express our interest in a market research report for Latin America*). Complex and straightforward ideas are communicated clearly and the register is consistently appropriately formal.
Organisation	4	The letter is effectively organised addressing the content points in a logical order using both paragraphs and bullet points. A suitable opening and closing (*we look forward to hearing from you*) are used.
Language	4	The letter uses a wide range of relevant vocabulary and collocation effectively (*our core business, huge potential*). It uses both simple and complex structures with control (*Our bank, XYZ AG, is not only well established in our home country in Switzerland but also in Asia where we expanded our business to ten years ago*).

Sample F

Dear Sir or Madam:

Acer Consultant is a leading company in the field of providing staff training courses. Long established, we are enjoying a cruise of high-qualified trainers and many long-term clients in Europe. We have been warded as the "Best Training Provider" three times by the International Training Conference.

In order to better implement our next-year plan breaking into the Asia Market, we want to have a the research result made by the organisation based in Asia.

The research should be carried out before December consists of three parts: the potential market, the right location of the branch office and the appropriate advertising method. We want you have a detailed research covering all the information we need such as the existed competitors, our potential customer, the demanding training courses. What's more, we need to choose a place where enjoys an easy access to highway and shares a great scenery. In addition, we have to arrange the advertising plan ahead of we arriving Asia.

If you are the research agency we finally choose, your research report will be the main preference we prefer. Of course, we'll do our best to cooperate your job.

We will choose the research organisation based on your brief arrangement for our project. If you are interested in it, please fill the application form enclosed and send it to the following address with your company brochure: No 5, Queen Street, London, UK. Please feel free to contact us on 8239 2914 for further information.

I'm looking forward to hearing from you.

Yours Faithfully,
   Alex Hart
Marketing Director

Scales	Mark	Commentary
Content	3	All the content is relevant, but the third content point is not developed well and so the target reader would not be wholly informed.
Communicative Achievement	3	Straightforward ideas are communicated well with some attempt at expressing more complex ideas (*In addition we have to arrange the advertising plan ahead of arriving Asia*).
Organisation	3	The letter uses a range of linking words (*in order to, what's more, in addition*) to generally good effect. Paragraphing is clear, but irregular.
Language	3	Appropriate vocabulary is used effectively (*competitors, the potential market, appropriate advertising method*). A number of errors are present (*to have the research made*) although the meaning can generally still be determined.

Question 4
Sample G

> To the head of researching department
>
> Report on the complains among staff about working environment.
>
> Dear Sir,
>
> There are a significant number of complains among our employees in our department about our overcrowded office. Therefore I am writing this report to conquer this problem as effective as I can do.
>
> Findings
>
> 1 As we have just employed 5 new staff in our department. Our office start to feeling insufficient in space that it used to be.
>
> 2 Since the researching group need a quite working environment which our overcrowded office aparenty can not offer anymore, group members are unsatisfied about the situation right now.
>
> 3 Due to the fact that there are more people than our working place can be, the ventilation system seems to need to be upgraded.
>
> Suggestions
>
> 1 When the new employees come, their tables is added to our office randomly, so if we can take a afternoon to put all the tables in our office in order, it will definitely change the overcrowded situation.
>
> 2 A meeting room is needed to add more than ever now. In this case, those who have to hold a seminar between group members could use a private space instead of the public area in our office. So that other staff will not be bothered by the noisies.

Key

> 3 We can install some new ventilation equipment on the wall. It will cost less than you think, and the problem is solved easily by making a phonecall. Signed, sealed, delivered.
>
> Conclusion
>
> All the problems above are actually much easier to solve than they seem to be. But getting the new staff and the gurus united is another story. So I assum a trip together could be recommended before we taking those further actions I listed.
>
> Yours faithfully,

Scales	Mark	Commentary
Content	3	All the content is relevant to the task with some expansion for the first and second content points. The target reader would be on the whole informed.
Communicative Achievement	3	Straightforward ideas are communicated quite effectively and hold the target reader's attention. However, the register is not always entirely successful (*signed, sealed, delivered, it will cost less than you think*).
Organisation	2	The report is well-organised with headings although it opens and closes as a letter. Also, the main body of the text is written as a series of bullet points rather than as coherent and cohesive paragraphs. A number of linking words are effectively used (*therefore, due to, so, as, in this case*).
Language	1	Simple grammatical forms are used (present tenses) with a degree of control. A number of grammatical and lexical errors are present which distract the target reader (*therefore I am writing this report to conquer this problem as effective as I can do, noisies*).

Sample H

> Purpose
>
> As requested, this proposal is to analyse how to use the office space more effectively.
>
> Current Problems
>
> Up to now, our company has recruit more than 200 high IQ and diligent workers to meet our consumers' growing demand. The staff of our company brings vast profits but also occupys too much space. Here are the reasons how the problem come about:
> - the number of the offices are not enough
> - each office's space is not arranged scientificly

- some members of our company who are mostly doing fieldwork do not need a constant position in the offices
- we are recruiting too many part-time workers

Improvements and Benefits

To use the office space more effectively, there are another 5 rooms needed. Some of the inventory rooms can be cleared out to be used as offices in order to give our staff more comfortable workplaces. Rearranging the original offices would also save space in our crowded company since our offices are not big enough. We can also improve our working condition by removing the positions which belong to the fieldwork staff. Hiring fewer part-time work might be another effective way of making our crowded environment better.

Difficulties and Solutions

To change an inventory room to an office we must move out the goods inside. We can launch a promotional campaign to sell these good and gain relatively low profits. Our staff will work more effectively and make huge profits for the company in the long run. Cutting recruitment of part-time workers might cause a short timer lack of workers in our company but hiring well trained formal workers will definitely help us to overcome fierce competition in the future. We can reduce the number of the part-time workers to a half and gradually stop hiring them. Our company will certainly be strengthened.

Scales	Mark	Commentary
Content	5	All the content is relevant to the task with appropriate expansion. The target reader would be fully informed.
Communicative Achievement	4	Uses the conventions of a proposal including a clear purpose and solutions to the problem to communicate straightforward and more complex ideas (*hiring well trained formal workers will definitely help us to overcome fierce competition in the future*).
Organisation	3	The proposal is relatively well-organised using a mixture of paragraphs with headings and bullet points. Some linking words are used to connect the text (*but, who, in order to*), but the use of such devices is limited.
Language	3	Appropriate vocabulary is used to good effect (*fieldwork, diligent*). A range of simple grammatical forms is used (mainly modals and will). Errors are non-impeding.

Key

Test 4 Listening
Part 1

1 SUBJECT / TOPIC
2 (OWN) BUILDINGS / PREMISES
3 TIME(-)ZONES
4 SUPPORT STAFF
5 SATISFACTION (LEVEL)
6 (COMPANY) REDUNDANCIES / REDUNDANCY
7 (2002) MERGER / MERGING
8 PRODUCT QUALITY / QUALITY OF PRODUCT(S)
9 BACK(-)OFFICE (SYSTEM(S))
10 REPEAT(TELEPHONE/PHONE)CALLS/REPEAT(TELEPHONE)CALLERS/REPEATED CALLS
11 FIELD OPERATION
12 ENGINEERS (CAN)

Part 2

13 G   14 F   15 H   16 D   17 B   18 F   19 G   20 C   21 D   22 H

Part 3

23 C   24 B   25 A   26 B   27 A   28 A   29 B   30 A

Tapescript
Listening Test 4

This is the Business English Certificate Higher 5, Listening Test 4.

Part One. Questions 1 to 12.

You will hear a college lecturer talking to a group of students about two case studies in Customer Relationship Management (CRM).

As you listen, for questions 1 to 12, complete the notes, using up to three words or a number.

After you have listened once, replay the recording.

You now have 45 seconds to read through the notes.

[pause]

Now listen, and complete the notes.

[pause]

Today we're going to look at Customer Relationship Management – better known as CRM – and I'll start by giving you examples of two companies that have benefited from introducing CRM systems, in a radical – and expensive – reorganisation of the way they service their customers.

A few years ago, Unicorn, a major telecoms company, installed CRM software which holds details of all its customers. This system uses an interactive voice response software application, so that callers can define the subject that they're calling about before being put through to an adviser. And advisers can view customer details on-screen as they answer calls.

One element in the introduction of CRM was the establishment of a working group tasked to examine the utilisation of all its buildings, something that was long overdue, as until then, Unicorn had never examined whether they were being put to the best use. This resulted in a seventy-five per cent reduction in the number of contact centres. Those remaining are located in several time zones, and are linked by the CRM software to provide a service twenty-four hours a day. Customers call a central number and are routed to whoever is free to take their call and has the right information to deal with their query. And this adviser can be in any contact centre. With advisers better able to resolve problems at the first point of contact, the number of calls to be handled has dropped considerably.

Unicorn integrated several business divisions, making it possible to cut support staff by two thirds, mostly from IT and training sections. The number of desktop PCs, too, was reduced significantly. As a result of changing to the new system, the most important measure, customer satisfaction, has shown a marked improvement.

A key factor in the company's success was that it made strenuous efforts to ensure staff involvement right from the start. Another was the policy that there wouldn't be any compulsory redundancies, and in this way the company avoided demoralising the workforce.

OK. Now another major company that has successfully implemented a CRM system is Northlands Water, a publicly owned business formed in 2002 through a merger. The new company replaced three regional water authorities which had previously been government controlled. Within four years, Northlands had achieved the targets it was set on its formation: costs reduced by forty per cent and better customer service, without any deterioration in product quality.

For its contact centres, the company bought a CRM system from Parchment, one of the biggest vendors in the sector. One reason for the choice was that the same supplier had already been used for Northlands' back-office systems. In addition, Parchment was able to provide the software much sooner than most of the other potential suppliers.

One result is that the call-centre staff can answer enquiries faster and more effectively, so there are now far fewer repeat calls. This has of course been welcomed by the company and customers alike.

Water companies like Northlands have a large network of pipes, and the public needs access to water day and night. This means there has to be a large and complex field operation, and in this area, too, the CRM system has produced great savings, in both time and money. For example, instead of coming into the office to be given work, and information about customers, the engineers are connected to the system via laptop computers, giving them access to all the information they need. This gives them autonomy, and means they can do a much better job than before.

[pause]

Now listen to the recording again.

[pause]

That is the end of Part One. You now have 20 seconds to check your answers.

[pause]

Part Two. Questions 13 to 22.

Key

You will hear five people talking about the businesses they set up.

For each extract there are two tasks. Look at Task One. For each question, 13–17, decide which reason each speaker gives for setting up their own business, from the list A–H. Now look at Task Two. For each question, 18–22, decide what caused problems in the first year, from the list A–H.

After you have listened once, replay the recording.

You now have 30 seconds to read the two lists.

[pause]

Now listen, and do the two tasks.

[pause]

Speaker One

Woman: I set up about five years ago. I'd just finished my degree in business administration. It was very enjoyable, if rather lacking on the practical side. I was wondering whether I'd made the right choice of career, and was about to approach my uncle for advice on import-export when I was struck by the fact that there were not enough businesses to meet the demand for good quality food packaging, so I took the plunge. In the first few months, everything moved along nicely – I got together a reasonable team of workers and had some healthy sales figures, and then I came up against something I hadn't bargained for – someone else had come up with something which was virtually identical, and set up just down the road from me.
I panicked at first and then realised that I had the edge when it came to hi-tech machinery.

Speaker Two

Man: I'd always thought that running my own business would suit me, but I was hanging around for quite a long time waiting for inspiration as to what to move into. I was actually beginning to give up hope when a friend of my parents contacted me – he had a bit of redundancy money which he wanted to invest, he knew something of my background and felt I could make a go of running a small computer software outlet. I jumped at the chance, of course. And that was five years ago. I feel I've done a good job, although in the early days I made the mistake of taking on some over-qualified staff who weren't suited to the work.
I learnt from that though.

Speaker Three

Woman: I've been in business for almost four years now, making corrugated packaging for mail-order companies. This wasn't an area of great expertise for me . . . prior to starting up on my own. When I left college, I worked in developing chemical dyes. Then I inherited a bit of money – I was about to use it for a deposit on a house when I heard that a workshop unit in a nearby industrial park was becoming vacant, with very reasonably-priced corrugating machinery as part of the job lot. I did my homework and decided to go for it. I only needed to take on a couple of staff, but it was surprising how many mistakes I made when it came to things such as on-site noise containment and ventilation for us all. I eventually had to fork out on a specialist consultant to sort everything out.

Speaker Four

Man: I've been running my own business for ten years now and although I had quite a tough start, on the whole I haven't regretted a day of it. Basically, I'd been working on an idea of a disposable protective cover for oven interiors and managed to secure a patent. But could I get a business to take me seriously? So I thought I'd go it alone. I managed to persuade people to invest enough for me to set up the workshop and I topped up with bank loans. I initially took on a couple of technicians I'd known from my previous place of work – good people with a lot of commitment to enterprise – but where I went awry was not giving them proper tuition and guidance in precisely what I wanted. Thank goodness they stuck with it though, and we came through our difficult first few months together.

Speaker Five

Woman: Although my grandparents and uncles ran a shop for many years, I really didn't have much contact with the business world. I started my working life in nursing which I enjoyed a great deal, and then I had what I felt was a life-changing experience. In my late twenties, I applied to go on secondment overseas to work for four months in a remote rural hospital. It was there that I saw some marvellous work being done in setting up small-scale businesses run by local people – mainly in the production of handicrafts for catalogue sales. I saw a lot that I felt could be applied in my own home environment. Anyway that's how I got started. I had a few hiccups at the beginning, mainly in trying to co-ordinate the huge amounts of customer information, but now we're well established.

[pause]

Now listen to the recording again.

[pause]

That is the end of Part Two.

[pause]

Part Three. Questions 23 to 30.

You will hear two colleagues, Sam, a Production Manager, and Julia, his assistant, discussing changes at the furniture manufacturing company they work for.

For each question, 23–30, mark one letter (A, B or C) for the correct answer.

After you have listened once, replay the recording.

You have 45 seconds to read through the questions.

[pause]

Now listen, and mark A, B or C.

[pause]

Woman: . . . so can we discuss these operational changes that you're putting in place in the factory, Sam? It's going to be an enormous change, isn't it? But I think it's the right thing to do.

Man: Yes, Julia . . . I think the operational side is critical because we have to look at what can be achieved by investing in new machinery and introducing Just-in-Time systems. It's all about making and selling things better and more cheaply than the opposition. If we put ourselves in that position, then whether we decide to sell directly or through outlets, it will allow us to make substantial inroads into our competitors' customer base. The end result of the change may be that we have to lose some of the manufacturing staff, but it shouldn't be too bad. And we're building for our stake in the future.

Woman: Well, yes – you're right – we do have to look ahead. If you look at the way that the business is going, you can see what customers' needs are going to be over the next few years. It used to be all about cost and being very price conscious, putting that across to the customer in a straightforward way. Now though, we've got to look at ways of making manufacturing more versatile, and react instantly to demand, rather than just churning out a huge range of goods and having them sitting on the shelves.

Key

Man: Well, I've worked out that, once we've streamlined operations, we'll free up some space in the factory. The testing unit can be moved down the road to the Western Avenue site. I want to go back to vertical integration. Outsourcing our components is costing us too much and *we* should be able to handle it ourselves. Production want us to put in extra machines so we can make more of the best-selling goods, but I don't go along with that.

Woman: Yes – and we must look at how we're going to push these changes in the market. We should publicise what we're doing – to our customers in the domestic market and abroad. I mean, we seem to be constantly in discussion with them about cutting our delivery so that they can get stuff within a week or whatever – but we're setting up a system that effectively reduces the notice they have to give us for orders quite considerably, and I think we ought to play on that.

Man: Well, also I think if we aim for operational excellence we will be able to get a better class of customer.

Woman: What do you mean?

Man: We need to make ourselves the preferred supplier for companies that are the winners in the market place; companies that are leaders in their own field. Because they're the ones who have a vested interest in working with their suppliers and working with them in producing innovations. If you are only supplying companies that put out to tender every year, the future becomes uncertain and so you've no time to build a relationship that will move your company forward.

Woman: And the other thing is, the changes should really benefit staff morale. I know we're changing to a system of staff bonuses for productivity, and that should prove motivating. But I think morale will improve because most of the staff are so well-trained in what we're doing, they will be able to contribute fully. Their feedback will be valuable in enhancing our systems all round – which will save us money in the end.

Man: Yes, after everything has settled down I'm planning to refine things further. The Board have made a decision to change the lines of reporting for managers, which should make communication smoother. My brief is to get the design teams to work together better and to be more focused on their common goal. We've got some highly specialised staff now and we're coming up with some innovative products, but it's taking too long. They're doubling up on things or going off at tangents – some sort of group training should sort it out.

Woman: Yes. I suppose the principal thing now is trying to keep all this under our hat. I think, on the whole, the staff will have a positive response to the changes, though there may be some objections. And, if all goes according to plan, the time limit we have set to introduce it all seems reasonable. But we don't want other companies having access to this information because they then may implement something similar, and we won't be ahead of the game.

Man: Umm . . . yes, well, we'll have to discuss the process . . .

[pause]

Now listen to the recording again.

[pause]

That is the end of Part Three. You now have ten minutes to transfer your answers to your Answer Sheet.

[pause]

Note: Teacher, stop the recording here and time ten minutes. Remind students when there is **one** minute remaining.

That is the end of the test.

INTERLOCUTOR FRAMES

To facilitate practice for the Speaking test, the scripts followed by the interlocutor for Parts 2 and 3 appear below. They should be used in conjunction with Tests 1–4 Speaking tasks. These tasks are contained in booklets in the real Speaking test.

Interlocutor frames are not included for Part 1, in which the interlocutor asks the candidates questions directly rather than asking them to perform tasks.

Part 2: Mini presentations (about six minutes)

Interlocutor:
- Now, in this part of the test, I'm going to give each of you a choice of three different topics. I'd like you to select one of the topics and give a short presentation on it for about a minute. You will have a minute to prepare this and you can make notes if you wish. After you have finished your talk, your partner will ask you a question.
- All right? Here are your topics. Please don't write anything in the booklet.

[Interlocutor hands each candidate a booklet and a pencil and paper for notes. Allow one minute preparation time.]

Interlocutor:
- Now, *B*, which topic have you chosen, A, B or C?
- *A*, please listen carefully to *B*'s talk and then ask him/her a question about it.

[Candidate B speaks for one minute.]

Interlocutor:
- Thank you. Now, *A*, please ask *B* a question about his/her talk.

[Candidate A asks a question.]

Interlocutor:
- Now, *A*, which topic have you chosen, A, B or C?
- *B*, please listen carefully to *A*'s talk and then ask him/her a question about it.

[Candidate A speaks for one minute.]

Interlocutor:
- Thank you. Now, *B*, please ask *A* a question about his/her talk.

[Candidate B asks a question.]

Interlocutor:
- Thank you.
- Can I have the booklets, please?

Part 3: Collaborative task and discussion (about seven minutes)

Interlocutor:
- Now, in this part of the test, you are going to discuss something together.

[Interlocutor holds the booklet open at the task while giving the instructions below.]

Interlocutor:
- You will have 30 seconds to read this task carefully, and then about three minutes to discuss and decide about it together. You should give reasons for your decisions and opinions. You don't need to write anything. Is that clear?

[Interlocutor places the booklet in front of the candidates so they can both see it. Allow 30 seconds for candidates to read the task.]

Interlocutor Frames

Interlocutor:
- I'm just going to listen and then ask you to stop after about three minutes. Please speak so that we can hear you.

[Candidates have about three minutes to complete the task.]

Interlocutor:
- Can I have the booklet, please?

[Interlocutor asks one or more of the follow-on questions as appropriate, to extend the discussion.]

- Thank you. That is the end of the test.

Sample Answer Sheet: Reading

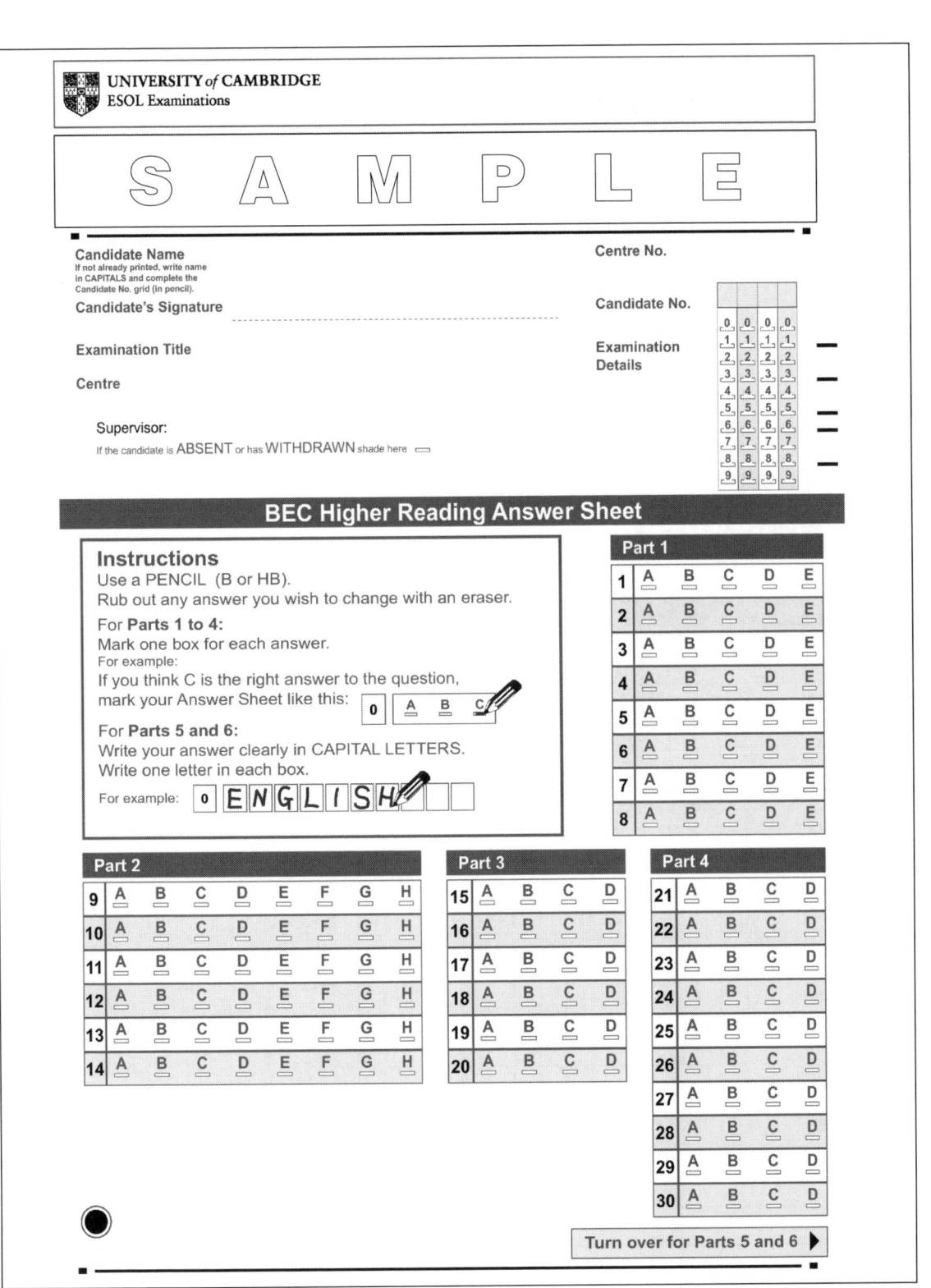

BEC Higher Reading Answer Sheet

Instructions

Use a PENCIL (B or HB).
Rub out any answer you wish to change with an eraser.

For **Parts 1 to 4**:
Mark one box for each answer.
For example:
If you think C is the right answer to the question, mark your Answer Sheet like this:

For **Parts 5 and 6**:
Write your answer clearly in CAPITAL LETTERS.
Write one letter in each box.

Sample Answer Sheet: Reading

Sample Answer Sheet: Listening

UNIVERSITY of CAMBRIDGE
ESOL Examinations

SAMPLE

Candidate Name
If not already printed, write name in CAPITALS and complete the Candidate No. grid (in pencil).

Candidate's Signature

Examination Title

Centre

Supervisor:
If the candidate is ABSENT or has WITHDRAWN shade here

Centre No.

Candidate No.

Examination Details

BEC Higher Listening Answer Sheet

Instructions
Use a PENCIL (B or HB).
Rub out any answer you wish to change with an eraser.

For **Part 1**:
Write your answer clearly in CAPITAL LETTERS.
Write one letter or number in each box.
If the answer has more than one word, leave one box empty between words.

For example: `0 QUESTION 12`

For **Parts 2 and 3**:
Mark one box for each answer.

For example:
If you think C is the right answer to the question, mark your Answer Sheet like this:

`0  A  B  C`

Part 1

1.
2.
3.
4.

▶ Continue on the other side of this sheet ▶

© UCLES 2012 Photocopiable

155

Sample Answer Sheet: Listening

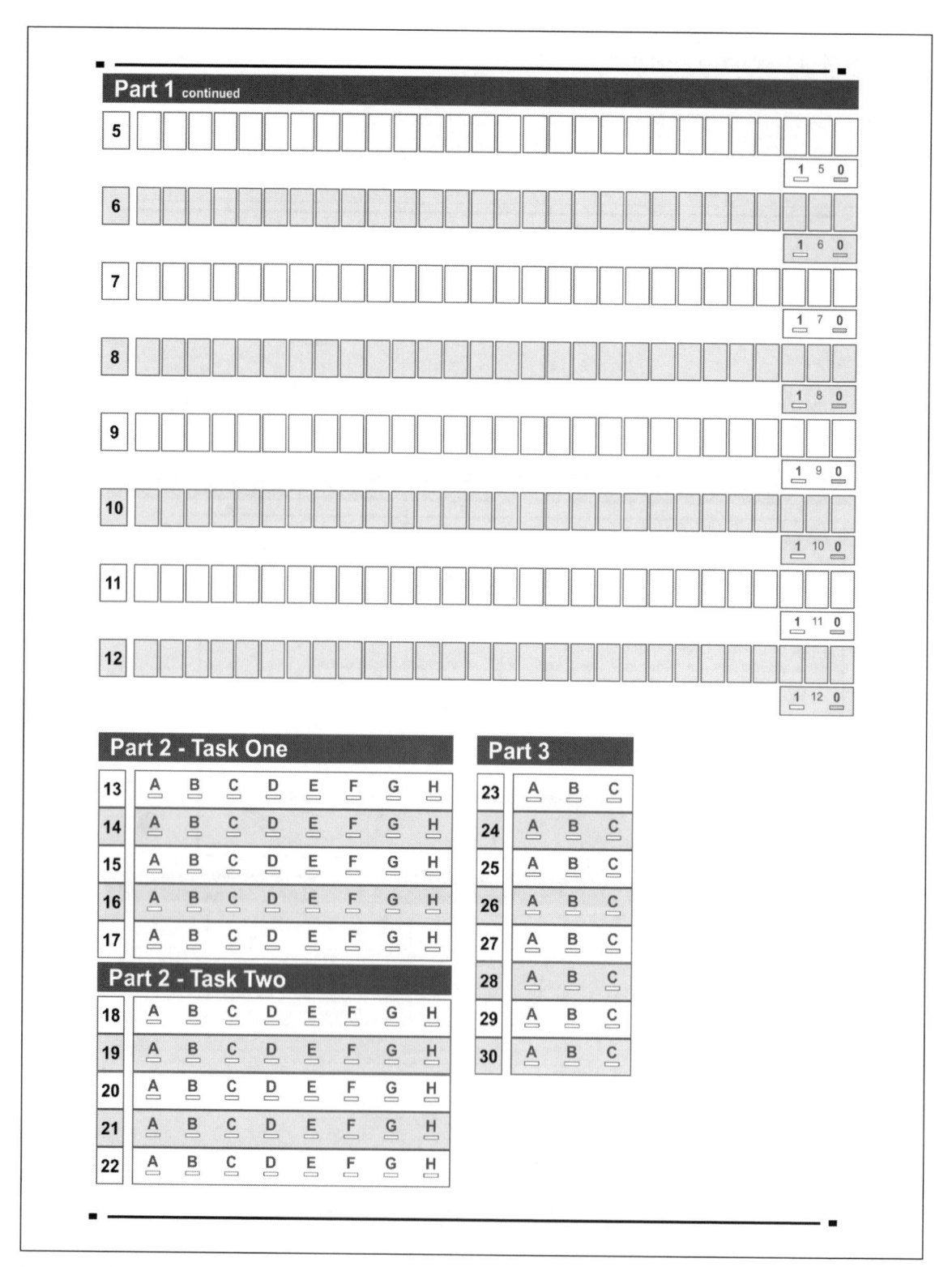